A LOT OF PEOPLE ARE SAYING

A Lot of People Are Saying

The New Conspiracism and the Assault on Democracy

Russell Muirhead

Nancy L. Rosenblum

With a new preface by the authors

PRINCETON UNIVERSITY PRESS

PRINCETON AND OXFORD

Published by Princeton University Press
41 William Street, Princeton, New Jersey 08540
6 Oxford Street, Woodstock, Oxfordshire OX20 1TR

press.princeton.edu

Library of Congress Control Number: 2019952090
First paperback printing, 2020
Paperback ISBN 9780691202259
Cloth ISBN 9780691188836

British Library Cataloging-in-Publication Data is available

Editorial: Rob Tempio and Matt Rohal
Production Editorial: Debbie Tegarden
Jacket/Cover Design: Sandra Friesen
Production: Jacquie Poirier
Publicity: James Schneider
Copyeditor: Ashley Moore

This book has been composed in Adobe Text Pro and Gotham

Printed in the United States of America

To Hazel and Leo Rosenblum Palmer and Alexander and Lila Muirhead

CONTENTS

This book is our account of the conspiracist thinking now enveloping political life. It struck us as something that could not be adequately understood as a "paranoid style" or as classic conspiracy theory. It is different—and more threatening. We came to call this conspiracism "conspiracy without the theory." It takes the form of bare assertion and innuendo. It dispenses with evidence and argument. It is embellished and spread through social media. And it is validated by sheer repetition: "a lot of people are saying."

Since we embarked on this project, conspiracists' charges have intensified and accelerated. Favorite targets are battered relentlessly, returned to again and again. Many come with the force of presidential pronouncement. "Rigged!"—the presidential election of 2016 was manipulated so that Trump lost the popular vote; then, the 2018 midterms were said—absent any evidence—also to have been rigged. As President Trump said, "There were a lot of close elections that were—they seem to, every single one of them went Democrat. If it was close, they say the Democrat—there's something going on, fella . . ." We have good reason to ask what this augurs for future elections—especially close ones. When elections are said to be tainted, will citizens accept official results? Can politics based on peaceful competition of rival parties survive?

When we wrote this book, our hope was that elected Republican representatives would use their partisan connection to speak out to persuade supporters that conspiracist concoctions were false and dangerous. That hope turns out to have been quixotic. Day in and day out officials endorse or indulge a steady deluge of malignant, unsupported conspiracy claims. Partisan loyalty and fear for electoral survival in a Trump-led party with a zealous base can explain a lot. Yet something more seems to be at work. Representatives have convinced themselves that they remain faithful to their oath and office, to constituents and country, even as they remain mute in the face of wild conspiracist charges. We have little evidence that they are roiled by the ethical failure to speak truth to conspiracism. As we see it, they have added self-delusion to cynical political calculation.

We stand by our judgment that conspiracy without the theory comes more often and with greater impact from the political right. While the left is rife with *conspiracy theory*—exhaustive accounts of the political influence of dark money or of Trump's collusion with Russian officials and oligarchs, for example—so far, the left has not been prone to the bare assertion that marks conspiracy without the theory. Conspiracy from the right owes to the flood of charges from the Oval Office by a president who claims to own reality; presidential conspiracism has unique power. We explain this political asymmetry too, in terms of congruence between conspiracists' delegitimation of a range of political institutions and the policy agenda of extreme conservatives. Even so, we expect that the demonstrated capacity of conspiracist claims to activate followers, and the temptation to answer fire with fire, means that this aberrant mode of politics is likely to spread.

Last, we anticipated that conspiracism would fuel violence. It has. The dehumanization at the heart of conspiracy fabulations like Pizzagate with its charge of pedophilia have a ghastly genealogy; the monstrous "other" is often cast as sexually perverse. We find that here. Hillary Clinton is not a fellow citizen or ordinary political opponent; she is an evil force. Once political opposition is delegitimized, the door is open to vigilantism by self-appointed defenders of the nation.

A follower of QAnon—the apocalyptic conspiracy claim that anticipates a cleansing "storm" that will return America to greatness—committed murder. And the El Paso shooter who killed twenty-two people, mostly Hispanics, in the summer of 2019 posted a screed linking his massacre to the charge that the "invasion" of migrants on the southern border was a conspiratorial plot to bring in illegal voters who would obliterate the right and eventually "replace" white national culture and identity. And interlaced throughout was a metaconspiracy of treasonous Democrats: "America can only be destroyed from inside out. If our country fails it will be the fault of traitors," the shooter wrote.

What does all this mean for democracy? The conspiracists' assault on common sense produces disorientation. It creates a deep polarization about what it means to know something— a divide more unbridgeable than partisan polarization, for it becomes impossible to persuade, compromise, and even to disagree. And conspiracism propels an ongoing, dynamic delegitimation of democratic institutions. When conspiracists strike at political parties—the defining institution of representative democracy—they subvert the idea of a legitimate opposition. As scholars who have argued for an appreciation of parties and partisanship, this is what first commanded our attention. It concerns us still.

Political theorists understand quite a lot about the origins of democratic legitimacy. We know less about today's unanticipated delegitimation of stable democracies. And we are on our own when it comes to the task before us—the relegitimation of foundational institutions.

We advocate a range of actions to defang conspiracism. All of them depend on the most effective antidote, common sense. Some may think that common sense is unstable ground for confronting a threat of this force. In fact it is formidable. For at every turn, conspiracy without the theory creates a distorted reality in which there are no verifiable facts. Conspiracism obscures our common moral horizon. Common sense discovers common factual ground. Appeals to common sense bring us back to who we are. They remind us that confidence in democratic institutions and democratic reform is well-placed. Common sense is what Thomas Paine appealed to in making the case for democratic revolution. And it is what democracy depends on still.

There are moments when we are startled into thought. Unanticipated threats have uncovered the fragility of democracy. One particular threat more than others seized our attention—what we call the new conspiracism. We have come to understand that conspiracism today is dangerous because it strikes at the basic institutions of democracy. But what startled us first was its power to disorient us. Conspiracism assaulted our understanding of reality. It insulted our common sense.

We wrote a few short articles in an attempt to understand what was happening. We asked ourselves, What makes the new conspiracism dangerous? What makes it new? Why now? Also, what is its appeal? And what can we do about it?

The subject required more detailed and thoughtful interpretation. We have looked closely at the thought of the president of the United States, the conspiracist in chief, and beyond him, at the full range of perverse charges that have become a regular feature of American politics.

We wrote this book to confront our own disorientation and recover our political equilibrium. We offer our account to others who are confused and disturbed by this malignant phenomenon distorting public life and endangering us all: the new conspiracism.

A LOT OF PEOPLE ARE SAYING

Introduction

The new conspiracism moved into the White House with the inauguration of Donald Trump as president of the United States in 2017. It seems that hardly a day goes by without a new charge of conspiracy, from "fake news" to "rigged elections," from "enemy of the people" to a "coup" perpetrated by the Department of Justice. Conspiracist thinking that was once on the margins of American political life now sits at its heart. No president—indeed, no national official—has resorted to accusations of conspiracy so instinctively, so frequently, and with such brio as Donald Trump.

Presidential conspiracism is unique; it is shaped by the character of the man and by the authority granted to the executive office. But Trump is only the most powerful and dangerous conspiracy monger. He shares a state of mind with those who invent conspiratorial charges and, using new broadcast technologies, disseminate them with astounding speed and reach. He is joined by many people, even his first national security adviser, Michael Flynn, who are drawn to conspiracist claims, assent to them, and pass them along;[1] by men and women in government who understand conspiracism's destructiveness but submit to it, thinking to use it to their political advantage; by the many elected representatives who acquiesce and remain silent; by civil servants who, deflected from their regular business, accommodate themselves to serving conspiracism's obscure purposes. Conspiracism has many adherents—some gullible, some sinister.

Conspiracy theory is not new, of course, but conspiracism today introduces something new—conspiracy *without* the theory. And the new conspiracism betrays a new destructive impulse: to delegitimate democracy.

Classic conspiracism—conspiracy *with* the theory—has not been displaced by the new conspiracism. Sometimes farfetched, sometimes accurate, and sometimes a vexing mix of the two, classic conspiracism tries to make sense of a disorderly and complicated world by insisting that powerful people control the course of events. In this way, for both people on the left and those on the right, classic conspiracism gives order and meaning to occurrences that, in their minds, defy standard or official explanations. The logic of classic conspiracism makes sense of things by imposing a version of proportionality: worldchanging events cannot happen because of the actions of a single obscure person or a string of senseless accidents. John F. Kennedy's assassination could not be the doing of a lone gunman. Lee Harvey Oswald acting alone could not defy the entire United States government and change the course of history.[2] The terrorist attacks of September 11, 2001, could not have been the work of nineteen men plotting in a remote corner of Afghanistan.

And in insisting that the truth is not on the surface, classic conspiracism engages in a sort of detective work.[3] Once all the facts—especially facts ominously withheld by reliable sources and omitted from official reports—are scrupulously amassed, a pattern of secret machinations emerges. The dots are woven into a comprehensive narrative of events. Warranted or not, classic conspiracism is conspiracy with a theory.

The new conspiracism is something different. There is no punctilious demand for proofs,[4] no exhaustive amassing of evidence, no dots revealed to form a pattern, no close examination of the operators plotting in the shadows. The new conspiracism dispenses with the burden of explanation. Instead, we have innuendo and verbal gesture: "A lot of people are saying . . ." Or we have bare assertion: "Rigged!"—a one-word exclamation that evokes fantastic schemes, sinister motives, and the awesome capacity to mobilize three million illegal voters to support Hillary Clinton for president. This is conspiracy without the theory.

What validates the new conspiracism is not evidence but repetition. When Trump tweeted the accusation that President Barack Obama had ordered the FBI to tap his phones in October before the 2016 election, no evidence of the charge was forthcoming. What mattered was not evidence but the number of retweets the president's post would enjoy: the more retweets, the more credible the charge.[5] Forwarding, reposting, retweeting, and "liking": these are how doubts are instilled and accusations are validated in the new media. The new conspiracism—all accusation, no evidence—substitutes social validation for scientific validation: if *a lot of people are saying* it, to use Trump's signature phrase, then it is true enough.

The effect of conspiracist thinking once it ceases to function as any sort of explanation is delegitimation. The new conspiracists seek not to correct those they accuse but to deny their standing in the political world to argue, explain, persuade, and decide. And from attacking malevolent individuals, conspiracists move on to assaulting institutions. Conspiracism corrodes the foundations of democracy.

Conspiracism's Targets

Our concern is not with every conspiracy claim. We leave aside narratives with only a tangential connection to politics: the 2017 charge that the CEO of Chobani, the yogurt manufacturer, smuggled immigrant rapists into the country, for example.[6] Such conspiratorial claims are always with us, tracking significant events. For example, the story that Neil Armstrong's walk on the moon was a NASA hoax designed to raise American prestige (the moon walk that people saw on television was a film directed by Stanley Kubrick, according to the conspiracy theory). Or the horrific conspiracist narrative that the 2012 massacre at Sandy Hook Elementary School in Newtown, Connecticut, was not real but rather staged by "crisis actors" or that it was a government inside job. And some conspiracist claims have no connection to politics, like the "chemtrails conspiracy," which claims that "airplanes are spraying a toxic mix of chemicals through contrails, with supposed goals ranging from weather to mind control."[7]

We focus on the catalog of accusations that go to the heart of regular democratic politics: rigged elections; secret plans by the federal government to use the military to abrogate states' rights or to seize guns; an illegitimate president who is not a native citizen; a secretary of state who "created" the terrorist group ISIS and conspires to weaken and humiliate America in the world; a "deep state" that sabotages the government.[8]

Amid this storm, the new conspiracists return to two targets again and again; we focus on them for the same reason conspiracists themselves do—because they are foundations of democracy: first, political parties, partisans, and the norm of legitimate opposition; and second, knowledge-producing institutions like the free press, the university, and expert communities within the government.

The new conspiracism has what we call a "partisan penumbra," an alignment with radical, antigovernment Republicans. Not all Republicans or conservatives join these ranks, but as we discuss in chapter 7, they rarely speak out against conspiracist claims. They exhibit partisan reticence. And while the Left participates in its share of classic conspiracy theories, it has not yet taken up the new conspiracism. What we have, then, is an alignment between the extremes of the Republican Party and the new conspiracism—a congruence founded in hostility toward government. These conspiracist claims persist in the United States even when Republicans themselves control government. Today, conspiracism is not, as we might expect, the last resort of permanent political losers but the first resort of winners.[9] Trump refuses to accept the terms of his own victory and incessantly conjures machinations against him, including coups d'état from within his own administration.

But partisan politics is far from the whole story. For what unites conspiracists is not ideological attachment to conservative causes or to the Republican Party but something deeper: disdain for political opposition, regulated party rivalry, and the democratic norm of "agreeing to disagree." Each conspiracist assault is specific to one candidate or policy or party, but it eventually extends to them all. It is not contained.

The other consistent target is the domain of expertise and knowledge-producing institutions. The new conspiracism rejects the specialized knowledge of congressional committees, government agencies, scientific advisory boards, government auditors, and civil servants in the Census Bureau. It discounts specialized knowledge outside government—scientists, social scientists, public health and education professionals, and any group, especially the free press, that serves as a watchdog alert to distortion in the flow of information and explanation.

The conspiracist rejection goes beyond the now familiar charge that a source of information is tainted by partisan bias. It goes further, to undermine the credibility of the whole swath of people and institutions that create, assess, and correct the universe of facts and arguments essential to reasoning about politics and policy (and everything else). Disdaining basic facts, the authority of expertise, and the integrity of knowledge-producing institutions, the new conspiracism is all encompassing. Again, the charges are cumulative: each conspiracy story has weight beyond its own particulars. The birther conspiracy, which turns on the claim that Obama's birth records were doctored, that he was actually born in Kenya and therefore was an illegitimate president, is a discrete charge about one government record and one person. But the blizzard of accusations, taken together, weakens the legitimacy of sources of knowledge and their role in regular processes of legislation and administration.

Conspiracism does not exist in a vacuum. It is one element among others that for decades have weakened democracy: "dark money," rabidly polarized political parties, alarming rises in social inequality and social insecurity, and more. And conspiracism is one element among others that have weakened the authority of knowledge-producing institutions: misinformation campaigns, and charges of "partisan bias" leveled at universities, research institutions, and publishing outlets. But the new conspiracism is a special kind of assault, and it poses a distinctive challenge beyond its specific targets. It is disturbing and dangerous because it is a direct, explicit, and wholesale attack on shared modes of understanding and explaining things in the political world. It unsettles the ground on which we argue, negotiate, compromise, and even disagree. It makes democracy unworkable—and ultimately it makes democracy seem unworthy.

Delegitimation

The new conspiracists claim to reveal odious plots against constitutional order, the fabric of society, national values, and national identity—but not for the sake of affirming any precise constitutional understanding or social order. Conspiracist charges claim that institutions, practices, policies, and political officials are malignant, but what exactly should be put in their place is unstated. Perhaps nothing at all. The new conspiracism is the pure face of negativity. Delegitimation is its product.

Delegitimation is not the equivalent of opposing, discrediting, undercutting, or sowing mistrust (though all this is conspiracists' handiwork as well). Delegitimation poses a unique threat to democracy: it rejects the meaning, value, and authority of democratic practices, institutions, and officials. Delegitimation is a process of falling away from the judgment that government has rightful authority. The people associated with these institutions, it is believed, no longer have standing to persuade or legislate, to reason or coerce, to lay claim to our consent or at least compliance.

The new conspiracism corrodes the legitimacy of democracy but does not hold up an alternative. There is no positive account of politics or justice in the background. It is not on the side of equality and it is not against equality. It is not on the side of tradition and it is not on the side of progress. In saying that the new conspiracism lacks political theory or ideology, we dissent from those who see a move to subvert democracy in order to transform it into something else—authoritarianism or protofascism or illiberal populism. For the company of conspiracists, there is no avowed and no discernable agenda of "regime change."

The new conspiracism is politically sterile. It is *de* all the way down: destabilizing, degrading, deconstructing, and finally delegitimating, without a countervailing constructive impulse. It is as if whatever rises from the detritus of democracy is less important and less exciting than calling out the catastrophes and humiliations wrought by the malignant agents who claim to represent us. We're witness to the fact that it does not take an alternative political ideology—communism, authoritarianism, theism, fascism, nativism—to delegitimate democracy. Angry, sterile conspiracism does the work.

Disorientation

The new conspiracism cannot be ignored or cabined off as simply quixotic or inconsequential. A part of us may step back and wonder at the sheer absurdity of this culture of conspiracy. Yet the insult to what we think of as political reality, to our common sense, is precisely what alerts us to danger. Our overriding response is anxiety and disorientation.

The allegations of the new conspiracism are often baffling and agitating, and we acknowledge at the outset conspiracism's intellectual and emotional toll. Bizarre and magnetic, coming at us with velocity, conspiracist charges compel the attention of reporters and commentators, social scientists and psychologists, and ordinary citizens. The attack on shared modes of understanding is fatiguing. The consequences of incessant charges of secret plots and nefarious plotters are political, but at the same time they affect us personally and individually.

Also unsettling is the knowledge that a large number of people assent to conspiracist charges.[10] Affirmations of conspiracy seem to envelop us—and not only because conspiracism has moved into the White House. More than half of Americans "consistently endorse some kind of conspiratorial narrative about a current political event or phenomenon."[11] It is as if conspiracy-minded officials and citizens suffer what the philosopher John Dewey called "a conscription of thought."[12]

The most striking feature of the new conspiracism is just this—its assault on reality. The new conspiracism strikes at what we think of as truth and the grounds of truth. It strikes at what it means to know something. The new conspiracism seeks to replace evidence, argument, and shared grounds of understanding with convoluted conjurings and bare assertions. Among the threats to democracy, only the new conspiracism does double damage: delegitimation and disorientation.

Some Conspiracies Are Real

Complicating our reaction to the new conspiracism is our recognition that conspiracies have sometimes been exposed in defense of democracy. Conspiracy theories have revealed the corruption of political officials in league with criminal forces and the covert machinations of hostile powers. By probing and uncovering the nefarious intentions and actions of agents opposed to the public welfare, conspiracy theory sometimes has been an instrument for reforming democratic politics. So we have good reasons not to dismiss the charge of conspiracy out of hand.

The detective work of classic conspiracism can reveal important truths about government that are otherwise covered up. Think of what it took to expose the actions of Michigan officials whose violation of public health guidelines allowed the lead poisoning of water in Flint, Michigan, in 2015. Their persistent stonewalling and denial increased the damage to public health. Despite their obstruction, over time the Environmental Protection Agency, doctors and researchers at hospitals and universities, and watchdog groups like the American Civil Liberties Union finally unravelled the truth about this act against the public and the conspiracy to cover it up.[13]

Sorting out what is plausible from what's not would be easier if all conspiracist claims could be dismissed as wholly unwarranted or as delusional. But there is nothing that makes conspiracy theories as such irrational or erroneous. To consult the recent history of actual governmental conspiracies—Iran-Contra, Watergate, or Tuskegee, for starters—is to confront the fact that "there are elements of treachery in the contemporary political and economic order."[14] Government officials do lie and do conspire, sometimes for what they see as protecting the public interest, often in the name of national security. For instance, after an exhaustive effort to uncover the truth about Osama Bin Laden's capture and killing in 2011, the *New York Times* reporter Jonathan Mahler concluded that the true account of those events may never be known because of the delicate American alliance with Pakistan. "The more sensitive the subject, the more likely the government will be to feed us untruths," Mahler says. "Of course, when enough people are obscuring the truth, the results can seem, well, conspiratorial."[15]

Distinguishing warranted from unwarranted conspiracist claims is further complicated by the way conspiracism aligns with partisan identity. Democrats are more likely to say that Trump colluded with Russia to cripple Hillary Clinton's campaign. Republicans are more likely to say that the media are manufacturing fake news to bring down the president.[16] We find ourselves navigating a political world buffeted by warring conspiracist claims. Is the miasma of conspiracism settling over politics wholesale? Is there a symmetry of untethered accusation launched from all sides?[17]

As we write, one set of claims has a grip on the nation's attention and has high stakes for our constitutional order. Robert Mueller, a special counsel appointed by the Justice Department, is investigating a massive conspiracy to breach national security and subvert American elections. Intelligence agencies have confirmed what is euphemistically called meddling in the presidential election of 2016. Russian actors hacked email accounts associated with Hillary Clinton's campaign and the Democratic National Committee with the goal of publicizing information that could assist Trump. Russian tactics also included staging rallies, targeting divisive messages to voters in closely contested districts, and exploiting social media platforms to urge African Americans to withhold votes for "Killary" Clinton.[18] The Mueller investigation also focuses on whether the Russian state conspired with individuals in the Trump campaign.

On the other side, Trump and his allies equivocate about whether they accept the known facts of Russian intervention. For example, John Bolton, appointed by Trump to be national security adviser in 2018, had earlier told Fox News, "It is not at all clear to me . . . that this hacking into the DNC and the RNC computers was not a false flag operation." It was, he suggested, possibly the work of the Obama administration.[19] New conspiracists charge that the investigation itself is a nefarious plot.

Special counsel Mueller is engaged in a "witch hunt," looking for something he knows in advance does not exist. In the most incendiary language, Trump's supporters cast the investigation as the entering wedge of a coup d'état.[20] And Republicans on the House Intelligence Committee ostensibly inquiring into Russian interference spin their own counternarrative in which Hillary Clinton's campaign—not Trump's—colluded with the Russians by gathering anti-Trump information and delivering it to a friendly FBI.

The warring charges have made many of us for whom conspiracist thinking is an entirely alien way of approaching politics veer toward classic conspiracy theory ourselves. Classic because it is not a matter of meeting "witch hunt!" with "treason!" but rather of connecting the dots, discerning the patterns, and constructing a narrative that makes sense of Trump's behavior toward Russian president Vladimir Putin—a narrative that makes sense of the refusal of many elected officials to "get to the bottom" of the Russia probe and guard against the dangers to national security.

There are no truth-in-advertising labels that tell us which conspiracist claims are warranted. There are no bright lines.[21] Some conspiracy theories are true, and some are false, and, increasingly, many are not theories at all. Confronted with a conspiracist claim, the question is, on one hand, whether we can set aside disbelief in the possibility of a conspiracy and entertain the charge and, on the other hand, whether we can set aside preconceived notions that agents are always out there, plotting with malignant intent. The question is how we assemble facts and draw inferences from those facts. When considering the possibility of conspiracy, do we consider contrary evidence and argument? Can we hold in mind facts that are in tension with one another? Can we maintain the capacity to acknowledge, for instance, that the same Centers for Disease Control that lied about the Tuskegee experiments (which pretended to offer free health care while deliberately withholding treatment from syphilis-infected African American sharecroppers) may not be lying when it publicizes proof that vaccines do not cause autism? Or that the CIA, which engaged in coups against foreign governments and experimented with LSD on its own unwitting agents, can contribute materially to an investigation of a conspiracy to defeat a presidential candidate?

Sorting out conspiracist claims requires willingness to entertain new information as it emerges. It requires a capacity for self-correction.[22] It requires resistance to resorting to round after round of spurious conspiracist counterclaims. If the Mueller probe finds no prosecutable evidence that the Trump campaign colluded with the Russians, would we say that the special counsel has shown himself to be party to a right-wing conspiracy? Or would we be open to the possibility that the Justice Department investigated the matter with integrity and did not find sufficient grounds to prosecute? Assessing conspiracist claims requires skepticism and common sense—both democratic virtues.

This Moment and Beyond

The delegitimation of fundamental political institutions and the disorientation that follows from the contest over who owns reality are grave developments. But they do not constitute a crisis—we are not at an inflection point where democracy is fatally undermined. We are not in transition to another form of government—to an authoritarian or radical populist regime. Delegitimation does not entail revolution or uprising; it does not have the shape of a sudden authoritarian coup. What, then, is the danger? Delegitimation hollows out democratic institutions little by little, day by day. It incapacitates and enervates democracy. It works slowly on democracy's foundations by eroding not just trust in institutions but their meaning, value, and authority. Combatting it requires identifying conspiracism for the threat it is.

We identify two responses to the new conspiracism. The first recourse is to call out conspiracists' claim to own reality. Speaking truth to conspiracy is a moral imperative—particularly for elected officials. Speaking truth can be effective, even if it is ineffective with respect to dedicated conspiracists. We can mitigate the corrosive effect of the new conspiracism if partisans of all stripes cooperate in speaking out, if watchful and engaged civil society groups and the media do their work, and if each of us serves as a witness by speaking out to family, friends, neighbors, and coworkers.

In addition to speaking truth, there is what we call "enacting democracy": the scrupulous and explicit adherence to the regular forms and processes of public decision-making. We are talking about a deliberate pedagogical response to the process of delegitimation. Enacting democracy makes government legible. That is, it gives citizens reasons to understand and appreciate the meaning and value of institutional integrity and ordinary democratic processes—exactly what the new conspiracism attacks.[23]

Reversing the damage means relegitimation. We can say with confidence only that it is a long haul requiring patience and stamina. For conspiracist claims have an extended half-life. The charges outlive discrediting by reliable sources, refutation of the claimed facts by experts, reports by bipartisan commissions, and Justice Department findings. And conspiracism is abetted by technological developments that add fuel and velocity to its claims. Moreover, these claims have evident appeal, both political and emotional. Still, we argue that delegitimation of democratic foundations is a danger we can meet.

Max Weber's 1919 treatise on politics as a vocation has long been a touchstone for thinking about political legitimacy.[24] The types of legitimacy and conditions for creating legitimate authority are well studied. *Delegitimation*, however, especially in presumptively stable, wealthy democracies, is barely studied at all.[25] Here we are on our own, confronting the unanticipated alien force we call the new conspiracism.

After Trump's presidency passes from the scene, the new conspiracism will remain. Yet if we do our work as honest witnesses speaking truth to conspiracy and demonstrate the integrity of core institutions, we will succeed in exiling conspiracists from public life and returning them to the realm of entertainment or to their natural habitat at the political fringe. In preparation, there is the work of understanding the danger.

THE NEW CONSPIRACISM

Let the frame of things disjoin.
SHAKESPEARE, *MACBETH* **(3.2.16)**

1

Conspiracy without the Theory

The United States has harbored real conspiracies, encouraged vigilance against would-be conspirators, and imagined conspiracy where there was none. During critical episodes in American history—in the early days of the republic, for example, and at the time of the Civil War—conspiracist stories shaped national crises. Great contesting forces each cast the other as an enemy of the Constitution and the nation. Conspiracy was the filter through which each side viewed the other. Real or imagined, conspiracism in the past took the form of conspiracy theory—that is, what we call "classic conspiracism."

In contrast, the new conspiracism is conspiracy without the theory. It sheds explanation, and it sheds political theory. We draw the distinction between classic conspiracy and the new conspiracism starkly not because every conspiracist claim falls neatly into one category or the other but rather because conspiracist claims that shed explanation and political theory have distinctive and destructive political effects: disorientation and delegitimation.

Classic conspiracy theory, whether it is true or not, tries to make sense of the political world. There are no accidents, no unintended consequences. As we mentioned in the introduction, classic conspiracism insists on proportionality and undertakes painstaking detective work: it is a kind of investigation that at least pretends to follow journalistic or even scientific standards.[1] The conspiracy theories about 9/11, for instance, revolve around the collection and interpretation of supposed facts left out of official reports and covered up by so-called reliable sources: errant facts about the Twin Towers' collapse, such as the temperature of burning jet fuel or the size of holes in the buildings. They strive to offer explanations that better fit these supposed facts—such as pilotless drone planes, even holograms that look like planes. And they fix on facts suggesting a cover-up, such as missing black box recorders or classified aspects of the 2004 9/11 Commission report. A visit to a website like Architects and Engineers for 9/11 Truth shows that classic conspiracism, with its effort to use standard epistemological methods to challenge official explanations, has not been superseded by the new conspiracism. "The official explanation of the failure" of the World Trade Center structure, the website says, "defies known scientific methods of analysis and is untenable in the face of logical investigation."[2] Once all the errant facts are scrupulously amassed, the thinking goes, we can understand the secret machinations that make sense of otherwise impenetrable events.[3]

The new conspiracist mind-set shares much with classic conspiracy theory. Both assume that things are not as they seem: malignant forces are at work beneath the surface.[4] Both insist that *right now* is the critical saving moment, so with any delay in exposing the nefarious design all could be lost. Both are a grim business. They warn of danger and they are themselves dangerous. But the differences outweigh the commonalities.

The Declaration of Independence and the Logic of Classic Conspiracism

The United States was born of a conspiracy theory about Britain's secret intention to extinguish liberty in North America. In the ubiquitous language of the eighteenth century, the revolutionaries resisted the British conspiracy to "enslave" America. If you read the Declaration of Independence on July 4, you are familiar with this earliest and most consequential American conspiracy theory, and with conspiracism in its classic form.

The Declaration is valued today for its inspiring avowal: "We hold these truths to be self-evident, that all men are created equal."[5] The authors were Enlightenment figures, confident that inalienable rights could be understood by anyone who exercised reason and attended to the message of Christianity. The truth of the conspiracy directed against the colonies' basic liberties, however, was *not* self-evident. The evidence had to be scrupulously laid out. The signers listed grievances against the Crown and broadcast them, drawing the attention of the world to the tyrannical plot and the imminent danger. In the view of American revolutionaries, a series of actions taken by the Crown, his ministers, parliament, and colonial governors were the dots that, once connected, formed a pattern. The grievances add up to "a long train of abuses and usurpations" all tending the same way—to reduce the colonies to "absolute despotism." The revolutionaries saw more than malign intent;

they saw planning, organization, and competence in the execution of the scheme. Those who doubted the conspiracy failed to comprehend the real, drastic meaning of these actions (or were Loyalists complicit in the plot). Finally, the Declaration directs a course of action: to dissolve the political bonds that connected them to Britain by armed resistance and to declare themselves independent states.

The historian Bernard Bailyn argues that the political consciousness of that time reflected a "hard-wired" disposition to interpret measures taken by the British administration as a ministerial conspiracy, as "evidence of nothing less than a deliberate assault launched surreptitiously by plotters against liberty both in England and in America."[6] By "hard-wired" Bailyn meant that "it was built into the political culture in eighteenth-century Britain and America"—a culture marked by long-standing Whig suspicion of government power—to see not merely "mistaken, or even evil, policies" but what appeared to be a despotic scheme.

The revolutionaries' conspiracy theory was "hard-wired" in a broader sense.[7] Historian Gordon Wood attributes the ready resort to conspiratorial explanations to a set of propositions about social reality shared by Enlightenment thinkers generally. These assumptions sited moral responsibility squarely in freely acting individuals and lent themselves to explanations in which intentions were the cause of events. If something important happened, it was because someone intended it to happen, though these intentions may have been concealed. American thought "was structured in such a way that conspiratorial explanations of complex events became normal, necessary, and rational."[8]

John Dickinson, an author of revolutionary tracts, is exemplary: "Acts that might by themselves have been upon many

considerations excused or extenuated derived contagious malignancy and odium from other acts with which they were connected. They were not regarded according to the simple force
of each but as parts of a system of oppression."[9] The pattern can
be deciphered to anticipate future actions; Alexander Hamilton predicted that Parliament meant to send "a large standing
army maintained out of our own pockets to be at the devotion
of our oppressors; the next step would be the martial law . . .
the abolition of trials by juries, the *Habeas Corpus* act, and
every other Bulwark of personal safety."[10] The political theorist Eric Nelson sums all this up succinctly: "A tiny tax on tea
is never simply a tiny tax on tea" but a "fatal precedent," "the
thin edge of the wedge."[11] And as Bailyn argues, the logic of
conspiracism was self-validating: "Once assumed, [the picture]
could not be easily dispelled; denial only confirmed it, since
what conspirators profess is not what they believe, the osten-
sible is not the real, and the real is deliberately malign."[12]

This is fully articulated, classic conspiracy theory, and the
declaration issued by the members of the Second Continental
Congress is not the only example. Historians have uncovered
nearly one hundred resolutions urging independence issued
throughout 1776 by states and counties and towns, artisan
and militia associations, and the provincial congresses of nine
colonies.[13] The tone, language, and form are consistent. In each,
a narrative of self-defense against enslavement is built from
fragmentary evidence. Each lists "abuses and usurpations" adding up to a tyrannical plot. These declarations also shared an
aim: to ensure that the war that had begun against the British
in 1775 resulted not in more petitions for a redress of grievances
over taxation or better representation in Parliament but rather
in independence. To see the conspiracy was to see the necessity of revolution. The authors delegitimized colonial political

arrangements and, importantly, linked independence to a fierce commitment to a constitutional republic.

The incendiary purpose of the conspiracy theory in the Declaration remains. On July 4, 2017, National Public Radio issued one hundred tweets that together contained the full text. Twitter followers identified as Donald Trump supporters were confused. They read the tweets as NPR instigating violence against the administration. "So NPR is calling for revolution. Interesting way to condone the violence while trying to sound 'patriotic.'" "Your implications are clear." "Glad you are being defunded. You have never been balanced on your show." And the omnipresent charge: "Fake news."[14]

Framing the Declaration as a conspiracy theory is to see it from only one—admittedly narrow—perspective and does not say all there is to say about the reasons to memorialize it. The Declaration is one of many instances of American conspiracism attached to major events—so many, in fact, that in his collection of conspiracist texts from the Revolution to 1971, historian David Brion Davis asks, "Is it possible that the circumstances of the Revolution conditioned Americans to think of resistance to a dark subversive force as the essential ingredient of national identity?"[15]

Shedding Explanation

The Declaration showed how the various abuses of Parliament and the Crown constituted in aggregate a settled design to extinguish liberty in North America: explanation was at the heart of the matter. The philosopher Brian Keeley says this is true for conspiracy theories in general: "A conspiracy theory is a proposed explanation of some historical event . . . in terms of the significant causal agency of a relatively small group of persons . . . acting in secret," which is to say, "a conspiracy theory deserves the appellation 'theory' because it proffers an *explanation* of the event in question."[16]

Yet the new conspiracism discards this defining purpose. Not only does the new conspiracism fail to offer explanations, there is often nothing to explain. Consider again the classic conspiracy theory that the US government helped plan and execute the 9/11 attack. However inaccurate, it helps explain the seemingly incredible fact that nineteen individuals unaffiliated with any state could successfully destroy the World Trade Center and attack the Pentagon.

In contrast, the new conspiracism sometimes seems to arise out of thin air, as with the claim that Hillary Clinton and her campaign chairman, John Podesta, ran a child molestation operation from the basement of a pizza parlor in Washington, DC (the "Pizzagate" conspiracy). Or that a routine military exercise in Texas in the summer of 2015 was the prelude to a national government take-over of the state (Operation Jade Helm, which we discuss at more length in chapter 7). The new conspiracists posit odious designs but not the how or why, and often not even the who. They do not marshal evidence, however implausible; there is no documentation of a long train of abuses all tending the same way. They do not make use of what Keeley calls the conspiracist's "chief tool," errant data.[17]

The typical form of the new conspiracism is bare assertion. Consider Trump's repeated insistence that busloads of fraudulent voters were sent to cast ballots against him in the New Hampshire presidential primary. The primary was "rigged." Yet there is nothing begging for explanation. Trump lost New Hampshire by fewer than 3,000 votes, true; but he won the election—a fact that nobody disputes. The outcome in the Electoral College would have been the same whether he won New

Hampshire or not. Unless one thinks it defies belief to suppose that Trump could lose an election, there is nothing here that needs to be explained. Nor are there stray facts to account for. There is no corroborating evidence of irregularity—not even one reported case of a fraudulent voter impersonating a registered voter—something that might get noticed in a small state where fewer than 750,000 people voted and many precincts contain fewer than 1,000 voters. The bare assertion "rigged" does not pretend to analyze how these alleged illegal voters were identified, rallied, and delivered to polling places, or how the plot was covered up.

Another example of sheer allegation is "birtherism." In referring to Barack Obama as the "quote 'president,'" there is no theory of when the hoax of his American citizenship originated, or how it was perpetrated, or who falsified documents, or why. The new conspiracism satisfies itself with a free-floating allegation disconnected from anything observable in the world. It offends common sense.

Today, "fake" is the most familiar example of bare assertion: fake news, fake FBI reports, fake government statistics, even fake weather reports exaggerating the strength of a hurricane. "Fake" is more than the charge that the report is untrue—it is shorthand for manipulation and fabrication to a purpose, done covertly. It points to a conspiracy. Fakeness is not a matter of error, after all, but of malignant intent. With every use of the term *fake*, conspiracists insist on the reality of a plot to make up news stories, concoct fictitious intelligence reports, and manufacture data—deliberately, not wantonly. And the conspiracist response is not correction or setting things straight; "fake" is the entire response. There is nothing more.

Sometimes the new conspiracism piles bare assertion on bare assertion. In its elaborateness, it can superficially mimic the qualities of classic conspiracy theory: connecting the dots and identifying patterns. As in, for instance, the QAnon conspiracy—a mash-up of new conspiracist charges, including Hillary Clinton's child sex-trafficking ring, a global network of Jews, and an inverted version of the Mueller investigation of Russian intervention in the 2016 presidential campaign. QAnon originated with an anonymous contributor ("Q") to the website 4chan who purported to be a government agent with inside information about Trump's master plan to stage a countercoup against the deep state. In its complexity, QAnon has the look of classic conspiracy theory, but it is a species apart. The new conspiracists are engaged in a fantasy decoding operation using scraps of intelligence (called crumbs) that pile bizarre elements on top of each other.[18] Not only does the theory fail to explain anything—it also lacks elementary coherence and defies common sense.

In addition to bare assertion, the new conspiracism takes the form of an ominous question—for example, those that followed the death of Supreme Court Justice Antonin Scalia: "How can the Marshal say without a thorough post mortem that he was not injected with an illegal substance that would simulate a heart attack," William O. Ritchie, a former homicide investigator for the Washington, DC, police, wrote in a Facebook post. "Did the US Marshal check for petechial hemorrhage in his eyes or under his lips that would suggest suffocation? Did the US Marshal smell his breath for any unusual odor that might suggest poisoning?" Ritchie suggested a conspiracy: "My gut tells me there is something fishy going on in Texas."[19] No specific accusations are made, and no falsifiable assertions are ventured. The "just asking questions tactic" substitutes for argument, evidence, and explanation.[20]

There is one more form the new conspiracism commonly takes: innuendo. In the 2016 campaign, Trump repeated a *National Enquirer* article that suggested a connection between

Senator Ted Cruz's father and John F. Kennedy's assassin, Lee Harvey Oswald. As Trump said, "Even if it isn't totally true, there's something there."[21] Or, as Representative Bryan Zollinger (R-ID) said about the allegation that Democratic Party officials had lured white nationalists and antifascist protesters to Charlottesville in 2017 in order to manufacture a violent clash, "I am not saying it is true, but I am suggesting that it is completely plausible."[22] The power of the new conspiracism is that it is satisfied with an allegation being "true enough," rather than true—which is the subject of chapter 2.

Shedding Political Theory

In addition to shedding explanation, the new conspiracism sheds political theory. It does not offer an account of what is threatened. It does not offer an account of the constructive political change that should follow from exposing the danger. Conspiracists have grievances, of course. They are powered by resentment and spite and righteous anger. But resentment and backlash are not a political theory.[23] The new conspiracism is agitating, attributing terrible meaning to seemingly ordinary actions and events, and at the same time politically sterile.

Conspiracists in the classic mode assume a protective pose not against this or that whisper, rumor, or cabal but against malignancy on a grand scale. They see conspiracy as the motive force in world events; indeed, history *is* conspiracy.[24] In this respect, classic conspiracism is often apocalyptic; at stake is nothing less than the survival of Protestantism threatened by a worldwide papacy, for example, or capitalism threatened by a worldwide communist movement. The new conspiracism, in contrast, lacks a sense of history, scope, or scale. The new conspiracism is not defending ultimate values; often the stakes are low, of the moment, and no values are articulated at all.

Classic conspiracism is embedded in a more or less explicit ideology or political theory. Nelson captures this astutely in his account of American revolutionary conspiracism: "Expect the worst from those in power" is a temper of mind, but what *is* the worst that we believe is being done to us? For that we need a conception of liberty, of law, of rights, of political institutions that are being subverted for conspiracy theory to attach itself to.[25] The Declaration of Independence, as we have seen, was itself a conspiracy theory in the context of a broader commitment to equality, natural rights, and government by consent. The sometime messianic claim of classic conspiracists to expose the threat and save the country or the world is inseparable from a story of just what is threatened and—crucially— from a vision of what the saved, restored, rehabilitated nation should be: a republic, a nation without slavery, democratic elections free of covert influence. Even the most apocalyptic warnings of disaster and destruction are attached to some vision of revivification and rebirth.

A high point of conspiracist thinking tethered to political theory was Progressivism in the late nineteenth century. The apparatus of political parties and the interests they served amounted to a system of corruption, collusion, and fraud, the argument went. Think party bosses, smoke-filled rooms, patronage and spoils, and voters not persuaded but bought. Progressives ferreted out the facts "all tending the same way," revealed patterns of corruption, and wove them into narratives of a covert combination of corporate monopolies and party bosses. We call it investigative reporting; they called it muckraking. The Progressives' purpose was to break up the corporate forces combining to subvert democracy and to wrest politics from political machines. In their place, they championed nonpartisan local government, reliance on expertise, and, above all, direct democratic participation. Progressives' conspiracy theory about schemes to capture democracy was inseparable from a theory of democracy. They had a political ideology and program of action.

The new conspiracism has no loyalty to any constitutional arrangement or program of political reform. To say that conspiracists have shed political theory is not to say that conspiracy narratives are walled off from partisan politics or without political consequences, clearly. But notwithstanding what we call the "partisan penumbra" in chapter 4, which aligns the new conspiracism with radical Republicans, the new conspiracist mind-set is not ideological. It is an exaggeration to say that "conspiracy theories have replaced ideologies at the heart of politics."[26] We only have to think of conflicts over taxation or health care to see that liberal and conservative, Left and Right, remain salient in politics. Yet the notion that conspiracism has replaced ideology does capture the fact that it lacks political theory, and its effects are wholly negative: disorientation and delegitimation.

Where classic conspiracism offers hopeful—sometimes utopian—accounts of what exposing the conspiracy can accomplish, the new conspiracism is not aspirational. Conspiracists offer no notion of what should replace the reviled parties, processes, and agencies of government once covert schemes are revealed. They are without political prescriptions or an ounce of utopianism. Even when the new conspiracism foresees an apocalyptic climax, as it does for Trump adviser Steve Bannon, there is no phoenix rising from the ashes.[27]

So conspiracists are not, in our view, agitating to transform democracy into something else—authoritarianism or protofascism or anti-liberal populism. There is no discernable agenda of "regime change." The new conspiracism is without any coherent constructive political aim. It is destructive—and it is politically sterile.

Shedding Collective Action

Absent political theory, another divergence from classic conspiracism follows: there is no call for collective action to free the nation from the malevolent design to subvert it. The new conspiracists imagine that the plotters they expose have an effective organization and an indomitable capacity for action. But they evidence none of that themselves. Classic conspiracism is prescriptive. The Declaration of Independence called for a war of independence. It directed a course of collective action: to dissolve the political bonds that connected the colonies to Britain, persist in armed resistance, and claim for the colonies the status of independent states. Similarly, Progressivism turned to building the apparatus of direct democracy.

But in the case of the new conspiracism, what should follow from bare assertion, innuendo, and ominous questions? Voter registration drives? Criminal indictments? Noncompliance? Violent resistance? We don't know, because there is no call to vote, litigate, resist, or arm. After the summary diagnosis of "Rigged" or "Something is happening here," there is a yawning hole where organized political action should be.

True, the new conspiracism comes with an aura of noncompliance with illegitimate authority. There is more than a hint of threat against the malignant opposition, including the press. Up to now, the new conspiracism has inspired only a few disconnected individuals to act, such as the North Carolina man who entered the Comet Ping Pong pizzeria in northwest

Washington, DC, and fired his assault rifle in an effort to "self-investigate" the child-trafficking charge he seized on from websites propagating the Pizzagate conspiracy.[28] While the new conspiracism does not prescribe collective action, the view that it produces "zombies" is too strong.[29]

Instead of collective action, the new conspiracists call for repeating and spreading their claims—"liking," tweeting, and forwarding. Repetition takes the place of organized political action. What Trump, for instance, wants is not the architecture of an organized political party or even an organized movement but a throng that assents to his account of reality. "You know what's important," he said about his fantasy of illegal Clinton votes, "millions of people agree with me when I say that."[30] Affirmation of his reality is the key act, as if by itself that is enough to collapse the globalists' world order, end "fake news" and "hoaxes," and repair humiliating national weakness.

This helps us understand just how the internet is vital for the new conspiracists and how their use of it is different from classic conspiracists'. For classic conspiracists, the internet is a source of dots and patterns—information that fills in the narrative and solidifies their explanation of events. For the new conspiracists, all the energy is directed at repetition and affirmation. Repetition is the new conspiracism's oxygen and, it sometimes seems, its whole purpose. With the internet, repeating charges takes no effort. Bare assertions are easily echoed and affirmed. Whereas explanation can be difficult, innuendo is simple. Even the character limit built into Twitter aligns with the new conspiracism's avoidance of evidence and explanation. The medium invites emphatic, unelaborated assertion.

Social networking is the stage for performing "a lot of people are saying," and for buttressing the claim by measuring the number of tweets, likes, and shares. The internet is the ideal medium for repetition and for signaling identification with others who spread conspiracist narratives. There are complications in trying to assess the scope of conspiracist claims solely by analyzing tweets and internet traffic. There are false accounts and fake sites and bots—programs that spread automated messages to a targeted audience, which accounted for 20 percent of the conversations about politics in the weeks before the election.[31] "What bots are doing is really getting this thing trending on Twitter," said one media analyst. "These bots are providing the online crowds that are providing legitimacy."[32]

Only Delegitimate

So, in its sheer negativity, operating unencumbered by political theory, ideology, programmatic aims, political organization, or a plan of action, where does the new conspiracism lead? It can do without political theory or ideology because its business is not protecting democracy, reforming democracy, or propelling transformation to another type of regime. Its product is delegitimation.

Here's what we mean. *Legitimacy* has two senses, philosophic and sociological. The philosophic sense asks what kind of a regime, in principle, would be worthy of support. The sociological sense asks whether citizens in fact view their political order as worthy of their support. The new conspiracists are not talking about legitimacy in the philosophic sense. They have neither a theory of government nor of justice that would tell us what kind of regime is worthy of support. The new conspiracism drains the sense that democratic government is legitimate without supplying any alternative standard. It operates at the level of citizens' attitudes and emotions, insisting that the defining elements of political order are not worthy of support. This is delegitimation—a process of falling off from an earlier judgment that government has rightful authority. Once having meaning, value, and authority for people, democratic institutions no longer do.

To be clear, delegitimation is not the same as mistrust. Mistrust of government is a perennial feature of democracy. It should be. It is an article of political faith that abuse of power is always a possibility and warrants vigilance. Rarely is undiluted trust possible, and nowhere in public life is it desirable.[33] Liberal democracy is designed to provide assurances, circumscribing authority by means of laws, institutional checks, mechanisms of accountability, and transparency. Within this constitutional setting, Americans are often mistrustful of what they see as an unjustified imposition on some area of personal freedom, privacy, property, religious expression, or dignity. Certainly, conspiracism inflames mistrust, and particular conspiracy claims pander to popular fears of abuse of power. But many forces contribute to mistrust of government today, among them the corrupt influence of "dark money" in elections, the sense that representatives are not serving constituents' needs or the national interest, and sheer incompetence in getting the public business done so that governing barely rises to the level of muddling through.

Political mistrust is typically targeted. It does not aim at institutions and political processes wholesale. And as long as mistrust turns on particular elements of government—the responsiveness of representatives, for example, or delivering what citizens need—it is corrigible. It can be repaired with the resources democratic institutions provide. Mistrust can be assuaged with less remote and more responsive representatives, for example, or by constraining the influence of private money in elections—in short, by a return to fairness and competence in areas that matter to citizens.

Even diffuse and widespread mistrust, which is a sign of anxiety about democracy, stops short of the judgment that government institutions and democratic politics have neither meaning nor value and are not authoritative. That is the difference. Where mistrust is a necessary element of democratic accountability and widespread mistrust is a sign of democratic failing, delegitimation is an active assault on democracy. Delegitimation exists when a political opposition that is mistrusted comes to be seen as a public enemy, for example.

We are learning what delegitimation looks like. Authorities are cast as hostile elements—worms in the bowels of the nation. Officials are "so-called" officials (for example, "the quote 'president'" Obama). They are demeaned and undermined, threatened, and declared criminal or traitorous. The set of assumptions undergirding regular and open political opposition and party competition is overturned. Knowledge-producing institutions and the information and reasoning they provide are rejected wholesale. Delegitimation drains authority from the institutions and practices that make democracy work.

And yet, again, the new conspiracists don't offer even a rudimentary account of what would be legitimate in the sociological sense—of what would invite citizens to see their government as basically fair. If legitimacy is understood more robustly, in its philosophic sense—as institutions and procedures that have authority because they produce just outcomes—the new conspiracism is seen to lack even a rudimentary theory of justice. All we have is this: institutions, practices, policies, and political officials are not what they seem, but what should be put in their place is undefined. Perhaps nothing at all. The motto of the new conspiracism might be "Only delegitimate."

The Russia Investigation

Let's look more closely at the Russia investigation, which lays bare the contours of the new conspiracism and its drive to delegitimate regular practice. In 2017 Robert Mueller, the special counsel, was tasked with investigating Russian interference in the presidential election to assist Trump's candidacy. From the outset, the White House and friends in Congress and in the media began a concerted campaign to delegitimate the investigation.

Initially, this took the form of an especially virulent partisan attack on the FBI and Mueller's team of career professionals. Never mind that principals at the Department of Justice were Republicans; the charge was that the special counsel team and officials at the FBI were Democrats and "politically motivated," incapable of objective consideration of the facts.[34] Kellyanne Conway, who serves as counselor to the president, put it this way: "The fix was in against Donald Trump from the beginning, and they were pro-Hillary. . . . They can't possibly be seen as objective or transparent or even-handed or fair."[35]

Over several months, the effort to delegitimate the special counsel's investigation changed from charges of partisan bias to a full-blown charge of conspiracy. Trump supporters began to use the term *coup*; banners on Fox News read, "A Coup in America?" On Fox News, Jeanine Pirro asserted that never in presidential election history had there been "as great a crime or as large a stain on our democracy than that committed by a criminal cabal in our FBI and the Department of Justice who think they know better than we who our president should be." Former Arkansas governor Mike Huckabee kept up the mantra in his newsletter and on Twitter, "It's an attempted coup d'état!"[36] Here is conspiracist delegitimation in a nutshell: a cabal within the FBI and Department of Justice was attempting to bring the president down.

The shift from partisan bias to full-blown conspiracy owes to the high drama surrounding an investigation that includes the president of the United States. Charges of political bias had become so anodyne as to lose impact; something more was needed. The shift is not simply tactical, though. The incessant infusion of conspiracist claims into public life had prepared many officials and citizens to receive the amped-up charge of an imminent coup d'état. Undeveloped, undocumented, and unreliably reported in a temper of unalloyed aggressiveness, this charge of a coup at the highest levels of government delegitimates the investigation. It also delegitimates central agencies of government like the Federal Bureau of Investigation and the Department of Justice. Ultimately, delegitimation envelops the government as a whole.

What Is the Appeal?

People are curious about what is hidden in politics—whether the private lives of public figures or the "real" story behind political events. The move from secrecy to revelation feeds this hunger. Conspiracism has this appeal. As historian Timothy Snyder cautions, the danger is that "discussion shifts from the public and the known to the secret and the unknown. Rather than trying to make sense of what is around us, we hunger for the next revelation."[37] The warning is particularly apt when it comes to the new conspiracism, for claims that things are not as they seem multiply wildly and opportunities to dive into the dark unknown are always right at hand in the media and via social networking. The new conspiracism, with its serial artificial crises, is exciting. It offers distraction from the tedious, frustrating, and often futile business of attending to known but difficult problems and political demands.

Curiosity, titillation, and entertainment aside, what is the appeal of bare assertion, innuendo, and ominous questions? Especially as it does not explain anything, what does the new conspiracism offer? Part of the appeal is performative aggression. The new conspiracism delivers dark claims, though the fabrications are erratic, vague, and undeveloped—more angry assertion than revelatory narrative. For angry minds it offers the immediate gratification of lashing out, of throwing verbal stones. It is a particularly gratifying form of vilification precisely because the more unfathomable the accusation, the greater the degree of disorientation, incredulity, and rage it provokes in its targets. Conspiracist accusations leave the rest of us, officials and citizens alike, baffled, our sense of reality threatened, our responses tentative and, it feels, inadequate. Disorientation is one of the dangerous effects of conspiracism, and producing this reaction is one of the new conspiracists' declared pleasures.

The new conspiracism also holds out the satisfaction of knowingness: "Accidents are planned, democracy is a sham, all faces are masks, all flags are false."[38] They are an elite, a "cognoscenti." Perhaps that is the wrong term, though, because *cognoscenti* has a prosaic meaning today: being particularly well informed about a particular subject. Conspiracists are more like the inner circle of an esoteric group or sect. But as we show, it is knowingness at low cost.

The new conspiracism's characteristic forms—bare assertion, ominous questions, and innuendo—are permissive. They have the appeal of elasticity and irresponsibility. Because of its vagueness, "a lot of people are saying" can embrace an expanding universe of conjured plots and public enemies. And "just asking questions" evades ownership of the claim. The author of any single conspiracist charge is often indeterminate; charges can arise spontaneously as a tease on a radio talk show or an anonymous throwaway on some fringe website. Regardless of whether conspiracists identify themselves or remain anonymous, a charge leveled without evidence that takes the form of vague innuendo avoids responsibility for what it asserts.[39] It suffices to announce, "I would love to know more. What I know is troubling enough."[40]

There is one more appeal: sheer negativity signals defiance. With their virulence and destructiveness, the new conspiracists, especially the president, assign themselves the status of outsiders. They are not politicians. They demonstrate that they are not devoted to the art of governing—which is welcome to those who think government itself is illegitimate. The defiance of norms conveys an antipolitical authenticity. It carries the promise to tear down the edifice and effect some indeterminate radical change. We see that there is an appetite for conspiracist delegitimation. At least until the consequences hit home.

Why Now?

We know that conspiracism is always present: there is always an occasion to suspect that, for pernicious reasons, things are not as they seem. Conspiracism has always had a foothold in certain domains of political culture, especially those at the outermost political fringe. But what explains the new conspiracism, and what makes it a political force?

Deep and long-standing discontents are at work in the background. There is the generalized antipathy to political elites, or the establishment, that marks a range of democracies on both sides of the Atlantic.

There is also the hostility to government that has characterized contemporary conservatism, for which the assertion, "Government is not the solution to our problem, government is the problem," has become a truism.[41] We look at this closely in chapter 4.

Social resentment and feelings of humiliation also fuel the new conspiracism. People are prone to target groups whom they imagine are responsible for a rash of grievances, and conspiracists call up and sharpen these inchoate sentiments and home in on targets of blame.

The dynamics that fuel populist upheavals are also at work in the new conspiracism. But at the same time, as we discuss in chapter 3, the new conspiracism is not reducible to populism. It is an independent force with distinctive delegitimating effects.

One force behind the emergence of the new conspiracism is plain: the revolution in broadcast technology that allows anyone to disseminate what he or she writes or says without any intermediary and at no cost. This has displaced the gatekeepers, the producers, editors, and scholars who decided what was worthy of dissemination. The way is opened for conspiracy entrepreneurs who initiate and disseminate a seemingly infinite array of wild accusations.

Our focus is less on the conditions for the new conspiracism than on its effects: delegitimation and disorientation in the political world. And these effects are possible because democratic institutions have already been weakened. For decades, party organizations and knowledge-producing institutions have been under assault. Long before the new conspiracism appeared, intensified political polarization had turned politics into a zero-sum game in which members of rival parties could scarcely cooperate or even agree to disagree. It had produced depictions of the mainstream press and the scientific community as skewed by political bias. This set the stage for the delegitimation of the party system itself. And it set the stage for rejecting the necessity of specialized knowledge for governing.

In chapter 2, we look at the logic of the new conspiracism. And we point to the political significance of the fact that what seems merely "true enough" is itself enough—enough reason to subscribe to conspiracist claims.

2

It's True Enough

Do people really believe that President Barack Obama was born in Africa? Do people truly think that Hillary Clinton and her campaign manager ran an international child sex-trafficking ring out of a pizzeria in Washington, DC? Or that the United States Army was planning to invade the state of Texas in the summer of 2015, declare martial law, and disarm the population?

We saw in chapter 1 that bare assertions, innuendo, and ominous questions are enough to get the new conspiracism going: as Trump said about the putative connection between Senator Ted Cruz's father and John F. Kennedy's assassin, Lee Harvey Oswald, "Even if it isn't totally true, there's something there."[1] And we saw Representative Bryan Zollinger perfectly capture the ethos of true-enoughness in his suggestion that the Democratic Party might very well have brought white nationalists to Charlottesville in 2017 to create a violent clash: "I am not saying it is true, but I am suggesting that it is completely plausible."[2]

The new conspiracism sets a low bar: if one cannot be certain that a belief is entirely false, with the emphasis on *entirely*, then it might be true—and that's true enough. This is the logic behind "Even if it's not totally true, there's something there." The new conspiracists do not necessarily believe what they say. But they do not disbelieve it either. As we have argued, classic conspiracy theory is about making sense of the world. But to assent in the way the new conspiracists do is something different. Their assent is forceful and has the stamp of certainty—the election was "rigged!" But when probed, the language of certainty often gives way to the language of "true enough." And "true enough" is good enough politically. Because the weak ground of assent does not cause hesitation or humility. It is not a barrier to publicly asserting emphatic claims about reality. It does not inhibit conspiracists from claiming to own reality. And for conspiracists in power, it is not an impediment to imposing their reality on the nation.

Classic conspiracy theories are often self-sealed systems of thought that, once one is on the inside, permit no exit; in this respect they can constitute a "crippled epistemology."[3] The new conspiracism too is a closed system. It is epistemologically flawed and self-validating in a different way, however. It is unconcerned with explanation and encourages assent to and action on the basis of claims that are not disproved and are not impossible, and are therefore "true enough." We will come back to this, but first let's look at whether aspects of the "crippled epistemology" associated with conspiracism are ones that to some extent we all share.

The Paranoid Style

There is a popular tendency to see all conspiracists as caught in the grips of irrational psychological forces. Conspiracy theories are often thought to reflect a paranoid state of mind—a connection that originated in the historian Richard Hofstadter's seminal essay, "The Paranoid Style in American Politics." But to categorize all conspiracy theory as "crazy" is to misunderstand both conspiracism and Hofstadter's argument.

For Hofstadter, "paranoid" is not a clinical diagnosis of individual mental disturbance. In his picture of conspiracism, conspiracists do not see themselves as singled out by a hostile world directing its animus specifically against them but rather see hostile forces directed "against a nation, a culture, a way of life." Hofstadter calls this style paranoid, he explains, "simply because no other word adequately evokes the qualities of heated exaggeration, suspiciousness, and conspiratorial fantasy that I have in mind."[4]

For Hofstadter, conspiracism arises from the tension between the belief that individuals shape history and the contemporary social-scientific view that large, impersonal forces shape history. As we saw in chapter 1, American revolutionaries saw events as entirely a reflection of the intentions of powerful individual actors. There was a moral coherence to their understanding of cause and effect in that they attributed desirable effects to good intentions and evil to bad intentions. The modern or social-scientific framework of explanation has shifted to impersonal forces and the aggregate actions of large numbers of people in politics, the economy, and society. The link between individual intention and consequence has been loosened. From the standpoint of contemporary assumptions about causality, conspiracists may appear, as they did to Hofstadter, as a retrograde minority in their insistence on the decisive force of agents with malignant intent. This insistence can seem like a distortion, one characterized in psychological terms as "paranoid."[5]

Hofstadter studied the appearance and effects of the "paranoid style" in American politics because he saw it as a threat to democracy. Conspiracism threatened what he saw as the moderate and pragmatic requirements of liberal democracy. Because of what they are up against, and because of what is at stake, conspiracists incline to secrecy and aggression. They reject mediation and compromise. Conspiracists, as Hofstadter saw them, are averse to "the manner of working politicians."[6] We agree with Hofstadter's assessment: the urgency that disdains any ordinary approach to politics as inadequate is something classic and new conspiracism share. Yet there is this difference: the new conspiracism not only is averse to the mundane workings of democratic politics but assaults its institutions and practices wholesale.

Normalizing Conspiracist Thought

Rather than pathologize it, Hofstadter insists that, despite his use of the term, the "paranoid style" characterizes "more or less normal people."[7] Today, a growing company of cognitive and social psychologists look at the epistemic processes that characterize conspiracism and see them as ordinary and universal.[8] In this view, conspiracism is not sui generis but rather an expression of basic thought processes that afflict all our thinking—"afflict" because these cognitive mechanisms, while ordinary, also invite error and distortions. Moreover, these built-in features of our minds are unconscious. We are not aware of the moves our mind directs us to make.

Three mental processes create the predisposition to see powerful hidden forces controlling events. First, we look for *intentionality* in events. People are averse to regarding anything of social and political importance as random, accidental, or unintended. It is an intolerably "absurdist image of the world to think that a series of coincidences changes the course of history."[9] In this respect, however convoluted its reasoning and evidence (or absence of evidence), conspiracism is simple, formulaic: the proposition that things are the deliberate work of powerful people is a constant. This is not to say that we correctly identify the agents responsible or their intention, only that we resist randomness and impersonal processes and unintended consequences. In his ruinous crusade to ferret out and expose Communist infiltrators, Senator Joseph McCarthy expressed the intentionality thesis to perfection: "How can we account for our present situation unless we believe that men high in this government are concerting to deliver us to disaster. This must be the product of a great conspiracy . . . a conspiracy of infamy."[10]

A second cognitive element is *proportionality*. When something of importance occurs, we look for a cause commensurate with the act.[11] We've noted this before: it seems implausible that events of world-historical importance could result from the actions of a single person or a few anonymous people. The effect (the destruction of the World Trade Center and the attack on the Pentagon on 9/11) and the cause (two dozen obscure individuals) seem out of proportion, so much so that one cannot seem to have resulted from the other. So, the conspiracist explanation goes, the US government must have been complicit in the collapse of the World Trade Center, just as the government must have been complicit in the killing of JFK— or, if not the US government, then the KGB, or the mob, or Fidel Castro in Cuba.

Taken together, intentionality and proportionality are mental assumptions that make conspiracism "far more coherent than the real world, since it leaves no room for mistakes, failures, or ambiguities."[12] The result is coherence at the expense of truth.

The third cognitive element behind conspiracism is *confirmation bias*. We look for facts that fit our preconceptions of how the world works. We assimilate new information that confirms what we already think and discard contradictory information. Confirmation bias propels us to harmonize what we hear and learn to what we know, or think we know. A standard illustration is the partisan differential in how people take in and interpret information. After Trump persistently trumpeted that "if you deduct the millions of people who voted illegally," he had actually won the popular vote, "a plurality of Republicans sa[id] President Donald Trump received more of the popular vote."[13] In this respect, a standard proposition holds that conspiracism is "largely a function of political attachment."[14] Other studies show that conspiracism is embraced by partisans of the Left and Right depending on who is in and who is out of power.[15] In one study, Democrats "who agreed on average with the conspiracy claims" proposed by researchers "increased from 27% before the election [of 2016] to 32% afterwards."[16] To take another example, Glenn Beck's radio show, which peddled charges of left-wing conspiracy, was popular when Democrats controlled the government in 2008; the show was canceled as irrelevant when Republicans regained control in 2010.[17]

Notice what follows from confirmation bias: insofar as conspiracism reflects one's political loyalties, factual correction of unwarranted conspiracism is bound to be very difficult. At least on some accounts, the attempts to correct misinformation can backfire; they *increase* the extent to which people believe erroneous information.[18] Even when corrections don't literally backfire, the repetition of conspiracist charges in the course of refuting them may nonetheless embed them in receptive minds. It is challenging for the media's reports and refutations to be effective. Thus, Trump's insistence that former president Obama had wiretapped Trump Tower has life that cannot be extinguished by the Justice Department's assertion that it was a total fabrication (the FBI and the Department of Justice's National Security Division "have no records related to wiretaps as described by the March 4, 2017 tweets").[19]

The disposition to look for intentionality and proportionality in explaining important events, not to mention the tendency to confirm our own biases, helps explain why conspiracism permeates all parts of American society and cuts across gender, age, race, income, political affiliation, educational level, and occupational status. An experiment that exposed people to a range of conspiratorial rumors (not all of them about politics) found that "over 70% of respondents expressed support for at least one of the statements," leading political scientist Adam Berinsky to conclude, "While some people hold mostly crazy beliefs, most people hold at least some crazy beliefs."[20] For instance, in August 2004, 49 percent of New York City residents believed that officials of the US government "knew in advance that attacks were planned on or around September 11, 2001, and that they consciously failed to act."[21] We can only imagine what the percentage would have been if President George W. Bush had insisted that elements within the government itself had planned the attacks. This is what is happening today: as a result of presidential conspiracism, about half of self-identified Republicans said they believe that American elections are "massively rigged."[22]

Our overview of general accounts of conspiracism— Hofstadter's paranoid style, cognitive accounts, and accounts that center on partisanship—would lead one to expect symmetry between conspiracism from the left and from the right. The standard proposition has it that parties out of power will be more inclined to conspiracy theories than parties in power, so that as parties alternate in office, we should expect to see conspiracism on both sides of the spectrum.[23] But with the new conspiracism, the symmetry we expect does not show up: the new conspiracism comes from the right, and it comes not only from those on the margins but also from those in power—from winners like Trump. There are other ways in which the new conspiracism diverges from the accounts we have just surveyed. Its bare assertions, innuendo, and bizarre fabulations introduce additional cognitive distortions. Accounts that normalize the general phenomenon of conspiracism obscure the novelty and the danger of the new conspiracism. Its danger brings us back to a distinctive element of the crippled epistemology that characterizes the new conspiracism: its tribalism.

The Tribal Basis of Assent

In classic conspiracism, belief has an evidentiary basis. Those who believe, for instance, that the government helped plan the 9/11 attacks cite observations and analyses to support their understanding. Evidentiary beliefs can be tested, in principle, at any rate—although, in practice, it can be difficult to test a theory that charges the government itself with wrongdoing when all the relevant information comes from the government. Yet the new conspiracism, as we have seen, proffers little evidence; there are few dots and patterns to latch onto. And the bar for assenting to conspiracist charges can be set very low: as we saw, to say that something is true enough, one can concede that it probably did not happen at all—but also that it might have happened. In the new conspiracism, this low bar is the standard: if something could have happened, even if there is no evidence for it at all, then it is true enough.[24]

When it comes to the political effects of the new conspiracism, what matters is not the epistemic basis of people's beliefs, but rather whether they assent to the conspiracist charge. As Christian theologians have argued, belief is an inward act of mind. Assent, by contrast, is something more public. We might assent to propositions even when we are not sure what we believe, even when our beliefs contradict what we assent to. While belief may have a high evidentiary bar, the basis for assent might be much lower—as it is for the new conspiracists.

It might have been that Obama's FBI tapped Trump's phones, as Trump claimed. And if it might have been, that's true enough—even without evidence to support the charge. For those who think it's true enough, what matters is that the hostile intent and capacity to commit the subterfuge were there. The logic of "true enough" breathes life into the new conspiracism as it corrodes standards of verification and validation. Consider the response to questions about Trump's tweet of a video that falsely purported to show a Muslim migrant committing an assault: the White House press secretary responded, "Whether it's a real video, the threat is real."[25] Because the world is one in which the claim could have been true, it is true enough.

From a philosophic standpoint, "true enough" is not a sufficiently demanding epistemic standard to ground justified beliefs; but the new conspiracists are not engaged in a rigorous effort to ground their beliefs in evidence. Which raises the question, Why assent to something in the absence of solid evidence? Understanding people's motives is a very difficult matter—motives are mixed. But it seems clear that part of the point of assenting to conspiracist fabulations is to communicate belonging. As a political phenomenon, the new conspiracism directs us to focus on the "we" that stands behind assent to claims like the election is "rigged."

The new conspiracism feeds off and in turn fuels a tribal mode of politics. To deny Trump's insistence that Obama wiretapped his offices is to disassociate from the company of those who attribute the worst to Obama and the Democrats. Assent to a conspiracy claim means the claim resonates with one's sense of the political world. A tribal belief is akin to Boston Red Sox fans' belief that the "Yankees suck." Such an assertion is not an affirmation of a proposition that is meant to correspond to facts in the world. Even if the Yankees were the best team in the world, for Red Sox fans, the statement "Yankees suck" remains valid because it reflects fans' identification with their team and each other. With respect to the Yankees, the question of justified belief does not arise for Red Sox fans, at least not in a philosophic or scientific way.[26] It arises from a tribal context, where validation comes from repetition by those in the relevant community—in this case, Red Sox Nation.

In the new conspiracism, narratives of secret, nefarious intent are emotionally compelling because of the way they fit with the affinities, connections, and hostilities that constitute elements of identity. As we observe it today, this fit is especially oriented to partisan identity.[27] Many more Trump voters than Clinton voters reject the claim that Russia tampered with vote tallies to swing the election to Trump. But many more Clinton voters than Trump voters reject the charge that millions of illegal votes were cast in 2016.[28] And even as late as 2017, more than half of Republicans purported to believe that Obama was born in Kenya (a belief that was very rare among Democrats).[29]

The political pay-off of "true enough" is substantial. The low epistemic standard—if it might have happened, that's true enough—allows conspiracists to assent to a distorted version of reality. Concretely, they assent to the proposition that Obama was born in Kenya because it might have been the case, however remote the likelihood. They then assert that he was born in Kenya. And conspiracists in power try to impose that compromised sense of reality on the rest of us. Assent to what seems "true enough" is what takes conspiracism out of the psychological domain and into politics. And it is what gives conspiracism the power to delegitimate.

Repetition over Validation

When it comes to true enough, what matters is not evidence but repetition. Participation in conspiracist social networks triggers assent. Echoing, repeating, sharing, liking, and forwarding a conspiracist claim is a show of affiliation with others who are angry and confident that things are not as they seem. Conspiracist narratives refresh these passions by reminding members of the group of what they feel with renewed energy. Several developments in communication help us fathom assent to these claims. Whereas many internet rumors "spike quickly and then fade out relatively quickly," alternative narratives that converge with politics linger, and have "sustained participation by a set group" of users. Someone looking to "validate" a particular conspiracist claim by checking different sites for confirmation will see the claim mirrored across the ecological niche he or she inhabits. Empirical evidence of the conspiracist "echo chamber" is mounting. The confirming experience is this: "a lot of people are saying."[30]

Conspiracist claims conform to what Jerome Bruner calls "narrative necessity."[31] They are required by the flow and consistency of the larger story; they are "subsumed to what is claimed to be the larger truth."[32] The Pizzagate conspiracy that charges Hillary Clinton and her campaign chairman, John Podesta, with running an international child sex-trafficking ring, for example, sustains the moral judgment of those who think the Clintons are so evil that nothing—not even sex trafficking in children—is beyond them. "Lock her up" and "Killary" signal a conviction that Hillary Clinton does unthinkably bad things and lies about them—the specifics are beside the point of the larger narrative.

Those who invoke "fake news" may not believe that every news story has in fact been fabricated in the way that Stephen Glass fabricated stories for the *New Republic* from scratch. It means that the "mainstream" press at outlets like the *New York Times*, the *Washington Post*, and CNN are hostile to Trump's presidency and perhaps also to conservatives and Republicans and to ordinary citizens who support the president.[33] Reporters could be in league to damage the administration, say, or in their support for globalism. The charge of "fake news" is true enough. Nearly half of Americans now say that the media fabricate stories about the president; the incessant charge "fake news" has taken hold.[34]

True enough conspiracist claims are not innocuous. Assent denigrates the conclusions of official investigations and the reliable media. When Trump's national security adviser, Michael Flynn, pleaded guilty to lying to the FBI, the president denied the confirmed fact of the matter: "Some people say [Flynn] lied and some people say he didn't lie. I mean, really, it turned out maybe he didn't lie."[35] The practical import of Trump's statement is to render the proposition that Flynn didn't lie true enough.

A steady dose of conspiracism encourages the disposition to see the worst intentions at work all the time, regardless of evidence. This has been called cynicism.[36] Still, it is not paralyzing cynicism. Assent to conspiracist claims represents a desire to join in a kind of political activity, albeit in a debased and sterile form.

Conspiracy Entrepreneurs

Those who buy into conspiracist accusations have their reasons for believing what they do. They are for the most part consumers of conspiratorial accusations, not inventors. They might repeat an accusation—or retweet it. But they are not the origins of the charge. Much of the new conspiracism originates with conspiracist entrepreneurs, ambitious people who peddle conspiracy in return for money, celebrity, and influence. Take Alex Jones, the Texas talk show host who was once among the most prominent producers of conspiracist narratives. (And a declared favorite of Trump.)[37] Conspiracism is a lucrative business, and Jones manufactures charges that he expects will be popular. His business is entertainment: he works to make his narratives titillating and persuasive. But he also wants political influence. He wants his audience to find his claims true enough—worth amplifying and repeating online in what has become a distinct form of political participation. Under pressure, Jones may concede that some of his claims, taken individually, are fabulations. He has been sued multiple times, including by families of the victims of the horrific 2012 school massacre at Sandy Hook for spreading the claim that the shooting was a false-flag attack and that the grieving parents were "crisis actors" hired to pretend to sorrow and loss.[38] Jones settled several civil cases brought against him, offering tepid apologies and retractions for "what [he] now understand[s] to be wrong."[39] But even the retraction of an individual item does not slow the production of new ones.

Or consider Stefanie MacWilliams, one of the propagators of the Pizzagate story: "I really have no regrets and it's honestly really grown our audience," she said. MacWilliams is confident that the truth will win out—the beauty of the internet is that people can crowdsource the truth—so she admits that she does not try to be "100 per cent accurate." Whether the Pizzagate conspiracy is true is an open question in her mind; the investigation by conspiracists is ongoing. "It's like a real-life Kennedy assassination where all the stuff is at your fingertips, and it's happening today," she says.[40]

Entrepreneurs are not restricted to people involved in conspiracy commerce. Take the example of the claim that the students from Marjory Stoneman Douglas High School who survived the mass shooting of seventeen of their classmates, and who spoke out in favor of gun control, were not real students. They were, according to the new conspiracism, FBI plants defending the bureau for its failure to catch the shooter. Or maybe something else: they were "crisis actors" who traveled to the sites of shootings to instigate fury against guns. The point of the new conspiracism is to create the possibility that they were not who they claimed to be—students who survived a mass killing.

These accusations reach a huge audience. They appear not only on sites like Jones's or in corners of the web but also in mainstream, right-wing media. They are reported by popular radio announcer Rush Limbaugh and by a guest on CNN, Jack Kingston, a former congressman from Georgia who, in the new conspiracist style of "just asking questions," said, "Do we really think—and I say this sincerely—do we really think 17-year-olds on their own are going to plan a nationwide rally?"[41]

The delegitimation of democratic institutions is possible because large numbers of people, most notably elected officials, adapt to a political world in which conspiracism is an element of identity and affiliation, and satisfy themselves if conspiracist charges seem true enough to repeat them, broadcast them, and invoke them when it comes to political decisions. In chapter 3 we look at the power of presidential conspiracism, and in chapter 4 we look at the problem of partisan reticence: congressional Republicans and other officials who acquiesce in conspiracist claims. Some officials are dedicated receivers and transmitters of conspiracist accusations, but many more are adapting to the malignant environment and to presidential conspiracism in particular. Partisan reticence inhibits speaking truth to conspiracism and stands as the most important enabling element behind a maelstrom of vicious charges and the delegitimation of democracy.

Scapegoating

Tribalism, we've said, fuels the new conspiracism. And tribalism is intimately related to scapegoating. The form scapegoating conspiracism takes is bare assertion, as when Trump declares, "The Mexican Government is forcing their most unwanted people into the United States . . . criminals, drug dealers, rapists."[42] The scapegoated targets of conspiracist charges are hated. They arouse animus and fury. The charge is simple: they bear responsibility for the nation's troubles. The origin of the term *scapegoat* is biblical—in a Mosaic ritual, one goat is chosen to be the symbolic carrier of the sins of the people.[43] Although scapegoating today is secular not religious, it bears the ancient traces of moral fervor and sanctimony.

Scapegoating conspiracism responds to resentment and feelings of powerlessness by singling out a segment of the population as the cause of cruelly disappointed expectations. Rapid social change and loss of social status render people ready to target a particular group as the cause of their misfortune. The humiliation of losing status, of losing economic security, of losing a sense of racial dominance and superiority all feed anger and the desire to blame. There is this, too: the humiliation of powerlessness—of being unnoticed and unheeded. And all of this has been deliberately inflicted by a cabal of malevolent elites and the undeserving groups they champion. So, where historians see long-term processes of social and demographic change, conspiracists see the handiwork of a despised group. These conspiracist formulations are simplistic and reductive. Scapegoating conspiracism is an "ideological misrecognition of power relations."[44]

In democracies, conspiracists have often fastened on secret groups for scapegoating. The reason is obvious: in an open society, any underground association suggests malicious intent. In the late eighteenth and early nineteenth centuries, Freemasons were charged with covertly controlling the press, manipulating the economy, and directing government. Everywhere, Jews are a favorite object of scapegoating conspiracism; the message of the forged *Protocols of the Elders of Zion*, published by Henry Ford, is repeated over and over, and it is with us still: the Jews are plotting to dominate the world. Conspiracists saw the papacy and Catholic priests as secretly working to weaken Protestantism. Conspiracists see the forces of atheism as threatening Judeo-Christian culture. Or they charge that Muslims are plotting to replace the Constitution with sharia law or to engage in terrorism. Just about any conspiracist cohort in the United States could adopt for itself the name of the late nineteenth-century anti-Catholic conspiracist group—the American Protective Association.

We've said that conspiracism conjures an explanation for grievances proportionate to indignity and resentment. And its satisfactions are aligned with the new conspiracism. Scapegoating conspiracism gives resentment a target. And scapegoating conspiracism is wholly negative. It does not offer an improvement in one's situation but rather the satisfaction of pulling others down. It expresses righteous anger. And like the new conspiracism, scapegoating can overcome lethargy. It is stimulating. It is a form of vicarious action.

Scapegoating can be combined with assaults on political opponents—clearly so when the opposition is cast as supporters of a despised group. We see Trump bringing three of his stock conspiracist claims together—scapegoating of Mexican immigrants, voter fraud, and the Democratic Party as a conspiratorial group aimed at destroying him and the nation. "Democrats are the problem," he tweeted. "They don't care about crime and want illegal immigrants, no matter how bad they may be, to pour into and infest our Country like MS-13. They can't win on their terrible policies, so they view them as potential voters!"[45] This is presidential conspiracism, unique in its destructive power. It is the subject of chapter 3.

3

Presidential Conspiracism

Presidential conspiracism is potent because the presidential office is itself so powerful. Executive authority has increased in response to national emergencies and presidential (and popular) frustration with Congress. As important, since Theodore Roosevelt and Woodrow Wilson, the American presidency has been a rhetorical presidency. The president is expected to speak directly to the people, to articulate a national purpose, to develop a legislative program, and to lead a party that carries the president's vision forward. Before Teddy Roosevelt, presidents were expected to be restrained and distant, more like guardians of the Constitution than like popular leaders. Over the course of the twentieth century, the latent rhetorical power of the office was liberated in the name of presidential leadership.[1] "Rhetorical power," as the political scientist Jeffrey Tulis says, "is a very special case of executive power. . . . It is a power itself."[2]

Presidents shape the national agenda and they also have the capacity to confer recognition: who is seen as a full participant in the life of the nation, what causes and which groups get seen and noticed and honored, which stories and explanations make sense of who we are and where we are going. So when conspiracism moves into the White House, it functions to divide the country against itself. Trump's conspiracism encourages people to disparage the ideal of national unity and to replace it with something more suspicious, more hateful, and more ferocious.

Of course, division, hatred, and violence are often center stage in politics. "The latent causes of faction," as James Madison wrote in the *Federalist*, no. 10, are "sown in the nature of man."[3] Nothing is more difficult in politics than bringing people together to cooperate for their mutual advantage. And bringing people together requires inspiring them to see themselves as a people, in spite of the differences of interest and identity that divide them. We see this at the founding, when the task of unification was so urgent. After remarking on the blessing of "one connected, fertile, wide spreading country" in the *Federalist*, no. 2, Publius (here, John Jay) wrote, "Providence has been pleased to give this one connected country to one united people—a people descended from the same ancestors, speaking the same language, professing the same religion, attached to the same principles of government, very similar in their manners and customs."[4] This description of identity was a misrepresentation then, as it is now—consciously so, as we know from reading Madison's *Federalist* essays on factions in America. Publius would have known that Catholics predominated in Maryland and Congregationalists in Massachusetts, the slave economy in Georgia and independent farmers in Maine.

But it was a misrepresentation designed to improve the country. The invocation of unity, which over time has been expanded to take account of minority groups and others who fell outside Jay's notion of unity based on similarity, has been a defining element of presidential leadership. At its most forceful, it brings people together by persuading them to embrace an ideal of unity that goes beyond what the contemporary facts might warrant. Every modern president before 2017 took some care not to turn one part of the people against another. "There is not a liberal America and a conservative America," Barack Obama said in the speech that made him a presidential contender. "There's the United States of America."[5]

By contrast, recall Donald Trump's campaign announcement speech: Mexico is "not sending their best. . . . They're bringing drugs. They're bringing crime. They're rapists."[6] Divisive conspiracism is a consistent feature of Trump's presidency. At a New Hampshire campaign stop in September 2015, Trump was asked about the Muslim "problem" in the United States and the "training camps growing where they [Muslims] want to kill us." The questioner was alluding to the rumor that Muslim communities in the US operate military camps to prepare members to conduct terrorist raids. Notwithstanding the absence of any evidence for the notion—and in spite of the fact that some Americans in the grips of the story have themselves plotted to attack Muslim communities[7]— Trump stoked the fear: "You know, a lot of people are saying that, and a lot of people are saying that bad things are happening out there. We're going to be looking at that and plenty of other things."[8]

The power of the president as commander in chief, as the one singularly responsible for identifying imminent existential threats to the nation, means that when the president scapegoats, it can seem patriotic to fear and hate and to act on these emotions. The president has the power to ratify scapegoating and normalize conspiracism—to render it a tool for politicians to use to attract support and sway opinion. Beyond that, presidential conspiracism becomes a rationale for degrading ordinary democratic institutions, creating what we will show is a "malignant normality."

Presidential conspiracism is doubly unique. Trump has unique personal characteristics, for one thing. For another, the presidency allows him to act on conspiracism in ways unique to the office, with incomparably destructive consequences. Conspiracism allied with presumptive authority and institutional power means that the president's claim to own reality is accompanied by the capacity to act on it. We are, in the words of poet C. K. Williams, "mortified by his absurd power."[9]

Conspiracism, Populist Style

It is tempting to identify conspiracism with populism. The combination is seen in Turkey, where President Recep Tayyip Erdoğan's narrative of an attempted coup against his government constituted a full-blown conspiracy theory that he leveraged to justify cracking down on opposition parties.[10] In the United Kingdom, the populist revolt against the European Union in the Brexit referendum was associated with conspiracism.[11] Conspiracism and a populist style come together as they do in Trump, but it is a mistake to see them as inextricably tied.[12] There are important differences. And conspiracism is an independent force with its own distinctive effects.

Although populism is an elusive label, we see a near-perfect expression of populism as a political style in Trump's campaign announcement screed against "Mexican rapists" and in his repeated rhetorical appeal to the real Americans: "The only important thing is the unification of the people," Trump says, "because the other people don't mean anything."[13] He has not disassociated himself from a radically exclusionary definition of those people who *do* mean something. Populism can be defined in precisely these terms—the political assumption that *the people* are a homogeneous, unified whole and that this "we" is being betrayed by a cabal of elites at home and globally.

Populists claim to channel the will of the people. Every political candidate and party speaks for some people, of course, but populists designate themselves the real people, the virtuous heart and soul of the nation, and they experience failure to recognize their status as an injury as real as any material harm—as a humiliation. The crux of populism, then, is insistence on the sole legitimate authority of the authentic, spontaneous "voice of the people." And populism may incline to suppress the residue, the alien fragments, the outsiders. Jan-Werner Müller puts what we call "holism" at the center of populism's "inner logic."[14] The title of an acute study of populism puts it succinctly: *Anti-pluralism*.[15]

Sometimes populism and conspiracism share the inner logic of antipluralism. As populism is about the vindication of the real people against elites, so conspiracism aims at exposing a cabal secretly plotting to betray the people. For his part, Trump casts himself not just as a preternaturally strong leader but as a defender of the people against these cabals. He rouses supporters not only by reminding them of his improbable victory but also by insisting that he remains the victim of an ongoing conspiracy. His daily communications with his followers are flush with charges of secret machinations directed at him personally and as president, and, by the transitive logic of identity, at them, "his" people. Conspiracism is, for him, at the crux of populist discourse and of presidential communications to the nation.

Populism and conspiracism come together in Trump in a way that is hard to unravel. Yet if Trump merges conspiracism and a populist style, the pairing is awkward. Looked at closely, the fit can be strained. Where populism lauds the unconstrained, untutored, intuitive voice of the people, the new conspiracists have a special power to see nefarious dealings that others don't. They have their own brand of elitism; they are a company of cognoscenti with special knowledge, identifying "false flags" and discerning the workings of a "deep state." They are members of an inner circle with a privileged ability to decode the hidden causes of things. They are not the spontaneous, intuitive people of populist ideology.

There is this difference too: nothing in populism entails an assault on argument, evidence, and common sense. One of the most striking features of the new conspiracism is precisely its assault on reality, which we discuss in chapter 6. Whatever its depreciation of constitutional constraints on the will of the majority or its dissatisfaction with the existing system of representation, populism does not seek to replace evidence, argument, and commonsense grounds of understanding with convoluted conjurings and unsupported assertions. Conspiracism is a distinctive threat, and it has distinctive effects that populism does not—delegitimation of democratic institutions and psychological disorientation. Political theorist Nadia Urbinati argues that populism, though hostile to political parties and to pluralism, remains within the confines of representative democracy.[16] It is tied to elections and committed to majoritarianism. Populists have always cast themselves as reformers. But the new conspiracism is not reformist. It has a purely destructive arc.

Trump's Presidential Conspiracism

Trump is the embodiment of the new conspiracism on frequent, sometimes daily, public display: the "deep state" planted a spy in his 2016 campaign; MSNBC host Joe Scarborough was involved in the death of one of his staffers; Justice Antonin Scalia might have been murdered ("They say they found a pillow on his face, which is a pretty unusual place to find a pillow"); and, of course, Obama was not born in the United States (Trump's investigators "can't believe what they're finding").[17] From the day Trump took office, conspiracism had a home in the White House. For example, early in 2017 a military-intelligence-style document circulated among members of his National Security Council and others close to the president. Titled "The Echo Chamber," the conspiracist document claimed to have uncovered a plan of "coordinated attacks" on the new administration's foreign policy carried out by a covert network of former aides to Obama operating out of a "war room."[18]

The president's conspiracism is sometimes imported, as it was in this case, but often it is his own invention, a reflection of his own sense of reality. This is its most dangerous aspect. Trump appears to live in the reality he has created by interpreting the world through his own personal needs. His unreality often seems, even to observers who are not professional psychologists, to answer to a drive to represent the world in a way that affirms his sense of himself—a combination of victimization and grandiosity (the target of "the biggest hoax in history"). His torrent of conspiracist claims—the National Park Service concealing the true size of his inaugural crowd; the masses of illegal voters casting ballots for Hillary Clinton in a rigged election—posits a reality conforming to powerful personal imperatives. His victory in the Electoral College could not be the whole story because it did not correspond to his conviction that his win was monumental—the widest margin in history; he seems not to have been able to confront the humbling fact that he had fewer votes than Hillary Clinton. When on January 19, 2018, Congress could not agree on a budget resolution and the federal government was shut down, Trump's comment was characteristically, breathtakingly self-referential: the Democrats orchestrated the crisis to detract from the anniversary of his inauguration![19] To his mind, the investigation into his campaign's possible collusion with Russians during the 2016 election is a "witch hunt." In dismissing or remaining silent in response to testimony of the chiefs of every intelligence agency, in demanding personal loyalty from federal law enforcement, the attorney general, the FBI, and the Special Counsel's Office, he demonstrates that the requirements of national security do not figure prominently in his reality.

All this is aligned with unashamed aggressiveness and invocations of violence—not just violent rhetoric but encouragement of actual physical harm. During the presidential campaign he expressed nostalgia for the "old days" when he would have been allowed to punch a protester in the face, and he offered to pay the legal fees of supporters who assaulted protesters. He also leveled this threat in connection with the possibility that Hillary Clinton would appoint a Supreme Court justice who would "essentially abolish the Second Amendment": "If she gets to pick her judges, nothing you can do folks. . . . Although the Second Amendment people—maybe there is, I don't know."[20] His accelerating attacks on the press have required news organizations to attach security guards to reporters covering his rallies.

Trump's conspiracism says a lot about him, personally: his cruelty and inclination to insult and cause pain, his recklessness, his impulsiveness, and his heedless failure to anticipate the consequences of his fabrications. It also speaks to the character of the new conspiracism, for Trump's mind-set fits with a way of thinking that does not admit the existence of an independent world recalcitrant to our desires and wishes. The birther example illustrates this. Trump pursued it relentlessly, indifferent to the fact of the matter. This was his entrée into politics, and he persisted in it throughout the campaign, with just one demurral when it seemed useful. The lingering charge in his mind is "true enough." Birtherism has become a touchstone for white identity politics, an element of tribal solidarity. But for understanding presidential conspiracism, the point is that it persists because Trump has no available source of knowledge other than what he imagines in the fierce, unceasing effort to assert his own reality. When a reporter asked him whom he talks with for information and advice, Trump was perfectly consistent: "The answer is me. Me. I talk to myself."[21]

The journalist Maria Konnikova has written that the frequency and seeming irrelevance of Trump's eruptions of "alternative facts" indicate that he lies "for the pure joy of it."[22] But his myriad falsehoods, although spontaneous, are not insouciant. And when it comes to conspiracism specifically, the pleasure principle is not in evidence, only explosive assertions of his own account of reality.

Truth, Lies, and the President's Claim to Own Reality

Liars do not claim to own reality. True, they lie and misrepresent a particular set of facts or events. But they assume and exploit a background condition of veracity. Liars do not create a reality wholesale; their goal is to deny a particular verity to achieve a particular purpose. Trump, like most people, tells useful lies, or tries to. Some of his lies are preposterous and easily refuted—for example, his claim that the *Access Hollywood* tape that recorded his boasts of sexual harassment was doctored. The same thing happened when, in an attempt to distance himself from his campaign manager, Paul Manafort, who was indicted and convicted on multiple criminal charges, Trump claimed, "He worked for me, what, for 49 days or something?"; the actual number was 144 days during a critical time in the run for the presidency.[23] A momentous instance occurred at the 2018 summit meeting with Russian president Vladimir Putin. Asked whether he accepted American intelligence reports that it was Russia that intervened in the 2016 election, Trump echoed Putin's denial: "I have President Putin. He just said it's not Russia. I will say this. I don't see any reason why it would be." Encountering outrage at home, he backpedaled, said he misspoke, and amended the record to read, "I don't see any reason why it *wouldn't* be Russia." This was widely characterized as a lie.

If Trump sometimes lies for the same reason everyone does, to protect himself and for some advantage, still, *lying* seems to be the wrong term to describe many of his speech acts. Better to say that he emits endless falsehoods and at an astonishing rate—every day for the first forty days of his presidency; over 3,000 falsehoods as of May 2018; 21 in one speech in Missouri.[24] A report in July 2018 documented the increasing frequency of his deviations from fact—going from making 4.9 false claims a day to making 6.5 a day.[25]

Liars want their lies to be believed as if they were the truth, but it is not clear that Trump cares whether his falsehoods are believed; he seems to care only that they are affirmed. He wants the power to make others assent to his version of reality. When Sean Spicer, Trump's first press secretary, said that Trump's inauguration had "the largest audience ever to witness an inauguration," he may not have intended for people to believe him, only to describe the world Trump wished for, and thus to enact Trump's own power. It was not a lie but rather an act of submission.

This is how the first president of the Czech Republic, Vaclav Havel, writing as a dissident in 1978, described the public speech of everyday life in Communist Czechoslovakia in his essay "The Power of the Powerless." Havel invokes a sign hung in the window of a corner store: "Workers of the World, Unite!" The grocer hung the sign in the window because the entity that delivered the fruits and vegetables dropped off this official sign, and the greengrocer did as he was supposed to. He put that sign in the window, Havel says, "simply because it has been done that way for years, because everybody does it, and because that is the way it has to be. If he were to refuse, there could be trouble."[26] In Havel's essay, the greengrocer's invocation of working-class unity was not about genuine conviction; the sign only conveyed that the storekeeper complied with authority. He submitted, as did the White House press secretary when he repeated Trump's assertion about the size of his inaugural crowd.

There is another way to try to characterize the claim to own reality, one that conforms to philosopher Harry Frankfurt's concept of bullshit, which he defines as an indifference to the truth or falsity of things.[27] In the myriad falsehoods he utters every day, Trump is manifestly indifferent to the truth of what he says. But his conspiracism is different. It is not bullshit. He is not blithely indifferent to the truth or falsity of his conspiracist claims. He presents an emphatic picture of political reality, and he cares very much that others affirm his reality.

The power to make people affirm the message is the power to impose reality. But brute facts are stubborn obstacles, as the philosopher Hannah Arendt argued. She illustrates the point by telling of French prime minister Georges Clemenceau's answer to a question about how future historians would assign guilt for the outbreak of World War I: "I know for certain that they will not say Belgium invaded Germany."[28] What Arendt calls brute facticity impedes those who want the power to remake the world according to their desires.

The question for politics is how politicians respond to the resistance facts impose on them. Trump wants to obliterate facts that frustrate his wishes and desires, and the new conspiracism is the tool he instinctively reaches for to create a new reality. For him, frustrating facts are not truths to be accommodated but rather fictions created by forces that conspire against him. Many of Trump's falsehoods come and go; they are reversed or dropped in the moment. But unlike the avalanche of lies and falsehoods, which hardly register before the next news cycle condemns them to oblivion, his conspiracist charges have long life. They are repeated over and over. His signature conspiracist claims do not die. In Trump's reality, Obama's presidency is illegitimate, busloads of fraudulent voters threw the New Hampshire presidential election, Trump's inauguration crowd was the largest ever, and the investigation into Russian assaults on American democracy is a witch hunt. Trump inhabits that made-up world. The pictures of what is happening, which serve his aggrandizement (or constitute his armor against humiliation), are the only pictures he can register.

There is no doubt about the consequences in any case: because of the rhetorical power of his office and his institutional capacity as president, his compromised relation to reality ascends from a private to a public condition. Because he is president, his conspiracism is not merely a concoction of his own private mind; it becomes a public thing. As president, Trump's conspiracist claims have initial authority, a moment of presumptive plausibility, that they would otherwise lack. Despite the astonishment and confusion that follow each fresh claim on the president's Twitter feed, his conspiracist accusations command attention and generate attempts to interpret them in a way that makes them coherent. All this comes with the office.

So Trump's conspiracist reality has consequences for our reality. It is something his supporters adopt and repeat, that officials in the White House and across the executive agencies are compelled to accept or to discreetly ignore, that Republican officials—almost to a person—acquiesce in a show of partisan reticence, and that thousands of civil servants and others must accommodate as they go about the now besieged and often distorted business of government. Trump imposes his reality on the country. That is the distinctive threat of the new conspiracism when it occupies the White House.

Creating "Malignant Normality"

Amplified by presidential power, conspiracism's cumulative effect is the long-term delegitimation of the institutions of American democracy. There is also the immediate distortion of these institutions as the president degrades them in the service of his conspiracist claims. On one hand, Trump's new conspiracism is gesture and innuendo, with no attempt to ascertain the truth of his claims, though as president in command of every part of the intelligence apparatus, he could. On the other hand, he commands officials and commandeers institutions to substantiate his reality. We have what psychiatrist and historian Robert Jay Lifton calls "malignant normality," where people accommodate themselves to distorted processes and inverted purposes.[29] In doing so, they make the malignant normal.

The feat of exploiting and corrupting critical institutions and the officials who run them is repeated over and over. The president accuses key government agencies of engaging in conspiracy and at the same time commissions them to affirm his charges and to expose and punish the alleged conspirators. "Uninhibited by the traditional protocols of his office, he makes the most incendiary assertions based on shreds of suspicion. . . . After setting off a public firestorm with no proof, he then calls for investigation to find the missing evidence."[30]

A story on Fox News gets Trump's immediate attention and he demands that the Justice Department investigate the Clinton Foundation, for example. Or, at the president's request, then–CIA director Mike Pompeo meets with William Binney, a conspiracist who suggests that the hack of Democratic National Committee emails was an inside job.[31] Congressional committees are recruited and special commissions are created to chase down Trump's claims that a specific conspiracy is in the works. He established a spurious Presidential Advisory Commission on Election Integrity charged, in effect, with confirming his claim that organized voter fraud cost him the popular vote. Its mandate was to engage in a "quixotic search for nonexistent evidence."[32] We have become familiar with the commandeering of institutions for conspiracist purposes and the manufacture of ad hoc arenas for "investigating" conspiracist allegations. The commission is a prime example of how conspiracist claims are now "making their way into the halls of Congress, and wasting the time of allies, intelligence officials and the FBI director."[33]

Conspiracism in power does double damage to democratic institutions and processes: it simultaneously denigrates them and enlists the very same debunked institutions to confirm conspiracist claims. That is, conspiracism simultaneously delegitimates and corrupts. Take Trump's unsupported accusation that Obama ordered the tapping of phone lines in Trump Tower. Trump charged congressional investigative committees with looking into this unsupportable tale of abuse of power. He enlisted Homeland Security secretary John Kelly to defend the claim as best he could on CNN, where Kelly said that "the president must have his reasons." As *New York Times* columnist Thomas Friedman wrote, "Then why doesn't the secretary of homeland security know them and why doesn't the president share them? And . . . why are you on television . . . saying the President has reasons but not saying what they are? That's how a morally bankrupt president soils everyone around him, even such a good man."[34]

A president who regularly attacks the press as purveyors of "fake news" and enemies of the people would have been extraordinary and is now routine. Yet malignant normality involves more than the routinization of unprecedented and destructive presidential language and behavior. We have malignant normality when the ordinary business of elected representatives, administrators, and civil servants is turned upside down or inverted inside out. Many in government accommodate and do what is demanded of them. The duty of executive branch officials is to serve the duly elected president, regardless of party or program. This obligation, which under ordinary circumstances supports the constitutional order, comes to threaten it. From the White House press secretary, whose job becomes endorsing the president's falsehoods, to the director of national intelligence, who cannot both serve the president and accurately report the threat Russia poses to American elections, malignant normality endows routine obligations with destructive consequences. Accommodation to malignant normality advances the momentum of delegitimation.

We see how the longer-term process of delegitimation goes: a conspiracist president tilts against his own government—against the Justice Department, the State Department, and potentially every agency he directs. Offended by the "deep state" that he imagines plots against him, the president first ignores and then eliminates the career bureaucrats who (in his mind) impede him. Initially, these agencies look illegitimate mostly to the company of conspiracists and the president's own base. Beleaguered, ignored, harried, and underfunded, the agencies—once staffed by professionals who responsibly served whatever party is in power—are progressively gutted and demoralized. As they lose competence and capacity, they will come to look more and more illegitimate to more and more people. The steady stream of conspiracist claims has cumulative force.

This is the uniqueness of presidential conspiracism: conspiracist accounts of reality can be realized. Processes ranging from information gathering to established norms of decision-making are cast aside as impediments to getting at the conspiracist truth of how things really are. Under conditions of malignant normality, what was once unthinkable becomes ordinary. And when that happens, it can become normal to assault the institutions on which democracy depends and make them look illegitimate.

Trump and the Parties

One institution on which democracy depends is political parties, and that is where delegitimation begins. In chapter 4 we will take an extended look at this process; we will show that the assault on parties amounts to a rejection of political pluralism and political opposition, and that the process of delegitimation turns on the charge that political candidates and parties themselves are conspiracies. Trump, who is both a conspiracist and an antipartisan, who is hostile to the critical place of parties in democracy, fuels this process.

Over most of his life, Trump was neither a Democrat nor a Republican. He campaigned for the Reform Party nomination in 1999 (hoping to enlist another television celebrity, Oprah Winfrey, as his vice presidential running mate). He considered challenging George W. Bush in 2004, saying on CNN, "In many cases I probably identify more as a Democrat."[35] He is an accidental partisan who opportunistically ran for president on the Republican ticket and confessed, "I'm not sure I got there through deep analysis. . . . When I give speeches sometimes I'll sign autographs and I'll get to talk to people and learn a lot about the party."[36] He ran against sixteen primary challengers, whom he gleefully emasculated. He won without the support of the national Republican leadership, party elites, or donors who were in anguish over his campaign, fearful that his dark, racist, and sexist rhetoric would be a long-term disaster for the party. He does not characterize his supporters as Republicans. One commentator described Trump as "the first independent to hold the presidency since the advent of the two-party system" 150 years ago. But "independent" is misleading if it suggests a centrist or moderate pose.[37] The political consultant Roger Stone put it in terms Trump would agree with: "He is bigger than the Republican Party."[38]

As president, Trump does not see the Republican Party—or any party—as the source of his power; hence his ephemeral alliances with Republican representatives and frequent attacks on both congressional Democrats and Republicans. He demeans leaders of both parties, including Senate majority leader Mitch McConnell: "Our leaders are stupid. Our politicians are stupid."[39] He campaigns against the reelection of sitting Republican senators, threatening their slim majority.[40] He feints at making "deals" with congressional Democrats. He exploits the deep division within the Republican Party—applauding the radical conservative caucus and obstructing the leadership's attempt at putting the factions of the party together in a way that would allow them, when they were the majority party in Congress, to govern. To the extent that Trump is interested in governing, he shows only sporadic interest in building an organization that can carry his policies and principles into the future. Seen this way, Trump is not, in fact, committed to governing at all. He has pet policies, which he tries to institute by executive order, but his own disinterest in governing and indifference to hiring people adept at administration often make a mash even of them.

This description of Trump as antiparty may sound startling, given that he has successfully recruited the allegiance of Republican voters. He does value the loyalty and affirmation of his supporters in the electorate. He encourages them to form a personal connection to him. In that way he has also tied the electoral fortunes of Republican candidates to his own. But he values the party only insofar as it is identified with him, not as a carrier of principles and programs that defined Republicans before him. Nor does he call the party to organize around new principles that could continue to define it after him.

Trump is consistent only in his inconsistency—his capricious passing preferences, his frustrations and reversals, and his conspiracist distortions of political reality. He leaves Republicans (and everyone else) flummoxed and at odds. One day, he urges members of Congress not to pass any immigration bill and rather to wait until after the midterm elections, when more Republicans will have been elected. Five days later, he urges—via an ALL CAPS tweet—those same members of Congress to pass a comprehensive immigration reform bill.[41] An organized Republican Party with a recognizable political identity may not survive his presidency. Indeed, the political commentator Charles Blow declares it already defunct: "The pre-Trump Republican Party is dead; the zombie Trump party now lives in its stead."[42]

This is the man and these are the circumstances under which the delegitimation of political parties is carried on. One way or another, Trump's presidency will come to an end—perhaps it will have ended by the time this book goes to press—but the disruptive force of conspiracism may not. What Trump has started, future presidents—not to mention members of Congress, senators, governors, and mayors—may emulate. He has made the new conspiracism a useful political practice and demonstrated its force. Moreover, neither the technology that fuels it nor the way repetition on social networks ("a lot of people are saying") validates it is going away. And there's this: we noted in chapter 1 that conspiracism is a stamp of being a political outsider willing to overturn the regular order. Future demagogues, if we allow them to rise, will not resist using it as a signal and a tool.

Trump is of interest as he directs our attention to the delegitimation of democratic foundations. In the next section we take a deep plunge into this process of delegitimation. We show why political parties and knowledge-producing institutions are foundational, why they are conspiracists' targets, and how delegitimation works.

DELEGITIMATING DEMOCRACY

They are yellow forms
Composed of curves
Bulging toward the base.
They are touched red.

They are not flat surfaces
Having curved outlines.
They are round
Tapering toward the top.
. . . .
The pears are not seen
As the observer wills.

WALLACE STEVENS, "STUDY OF TWO PEARS"

4

Political Parties

Conspiracist claims have traveled from the margins of political life to the White House, and with presidential power come unique dangers. We have described this alarming shift. We have given it a name—the new conspiracism—and identified its divergence from classic conspiracy theory. And we have signaled its malignant effects—the delegitimation of democratic institutions and the disorientation of many citizens. Conspiracism sows mistrust, degrades political reasoning, and wrecks the forms and terms of ordinary political disagreement. It is a potent force that subverts democracy's meaning, value, and authority.

The new conspiracism's targets are not arbitrary. They are democracy's critical foundations. The targets are key institutions and epistemological foundations as well, meaning "ways of knowing" that make democratic government and politics possible. Grasping the danger also entails explaining *how* the process of delegitimating these foundations actually works. Our initial look at the new conspiracism from a perch high off the ground is a start. Here and in chapter 5 we take a deep plunge into conspiracist delegitimation, and in chapter 6 we look in detail at the experience of disorientation.

The new conspiracists spew attacks, expressing not only long-held grievances but also innumerable others as they arise and reveling in the outrage their claims generate. But while it may seem quixotic and diffuse, the new conspiracism consistently circles around an identifiable set of targets: political parties and knowledge-producing institutions. What makes the attack on *these* elements of democracy so dangerous? The answer is that parties and elections, on one hand, and the administrative state dependent on expert knowledge, on the other hand, are two foundations of democratic government. Neither democratic politics nor governing can be carried on without them; as a practical, operational matter, both are essential. They are also foundational in another sense: they provide twin grounds of democratic legitimacy. As philosopher Pierre Rosanvallon puts it, there is "an inescapable dualism" to democracy; "it has to arrange for periodic choice among significantly different individuals and programs, and it must establish institutions that rise above those differences to promote the general interest."[1]

Political representation via contested elections organized by parties is the formal defining characteristic of modern democracy. Parties, partisanship, and elections are where interests, opinions, judgments, and values are shaped and come into conflict. Representatives are selected in a process of regulated party rivalry. Parties and partisanship are the direct institutional expression of social and political pluralism and of the fact that, in democracy, opposition is expected and legitimate.

A second foundation of democracy is epistemic: modern democracy depends on expert knowledge. This comes to bear especially in what has come to be called the administrative state, which comprises the myriad agencies staffed by career professionals who rely on specialized knowledge they create or draw on from research institutions and from civil society groups outside government. This is the basis for formulating, implementing, and enforcing public policy touching everything from safe water to consumer protection to interest rates and banking rules. These scientists, statisticians, economists, and ethicists are not elected; they are insulated to a reasonable extent from political controversies and partisan influence. They are "disinterested" as a matter of professional discipline and seek to apply impartial standards in the general interest.

In this section, we focus on the moral and political value of these twin foundations of democracy, and we show how the process of delegitimation works. We plunge into the grim details of conspiracist assaults on parties and partisanship and on knowledge-producing institutions, beginning in this chapter with parties.

Parties and Representative Democracy

Among conspiracists' targets, the assault on political parties is not occasional but incessant, and it aligns with a long-standing American antipathy to parties and partisans. Despite being the defining institution of representative democracy—in the formal political science definition, democracy is a system in which two or more parties compete for the popular vote in free and fair elections—parties and partisanship are commonly maligned. Aversion does not always take the extreme form of claiming that parties are conspiracies, but that is what we have today. This characterization is crucial, for the delegitimation of parties that proceeds by classifying them as conspiracies should be understood as an attack on democracy. Because antipathy toward parties and partisans is commonplace, we don't as readily spring to their defense today as we do, for example, to the defense of the FBI or CIA against attacks that *they* harbor conspiracies. To understand why the conspiracist attack on parties is an attack on democracy, we need to understand why parties are critical and irreplaceable democratic institutions.

Without political parties, democracy takes a radically populist form.[2] The one, homogeneous, "true" people stand behind their leader without the party as an intermediary institution. Populism is, as we have argued, antipluralist. And, for their part, parties are the institutional expression and guarantors of political pluralism. They connect the natural pluralism of a free society—churches, clubs, interest groups, civic associations—with the formal institutions of government. They connect candidates and programs to the loyalties and interests of citizens. The relation is reciprocal: parties bring the doings of the national government within the sightlines of citizens.[3]

Parties are essential to representative democracy in pragmatic ways: selecting candidates, forming majorities, organizing legislatures, and providing the glue across state and national politics. There is also a demonstrable relationship between partisanship and high levels of voter participation.[4] But, beyond the pragmatic things that parties do for democracy, there is this fundamental thing: parties translate the pluralism of society into organized political conflict. They do the work of drawing politically relevant lines of division and shaping the system of conflict that orders democratic politics and decision-making. Parties are not simply reflections of disagreements and conflicts that exist independent of politics. Parties and partisans organize conflict in the process of creating coalitions.[5]

Party competition is constitutive. It creates a system of conflict. It "stages the battle." An astute theorist of parties, Maurice Duverger, captures the creative aspect of translating pluralism into politics through metaphors of natural and artistic creation: parties crystallize, coagulate, synthesize, smooth down, and mold.[6] Creativity in politics is rarely recognized, and when it is, the focus is on founding moments or constitutional design, transformative social movements or revolution—not on "normal politics."[7] Yet everyday democratic politics requires creativity and political ingenuity because neither "the people" nor "the majority" nor the "opposition" exists on its own. Parties make democracy happen.

The creative role of parties means that in one respect the traditional complaint about parties is correct: parties *do* challenge the imagined unity or holism of the political order. On one hand, political parties seek to bring people together in majority coalitions to govern. On the other, they create and exacerbate divisions. Indeed, partiality and opposition are their raison d'être. While parties at their best are oriented to a conception of the common good, they nonetheless always stand for a part rather than the whole.

Parties also create partisans—citizens who identify with a party. Partisanship is the political identity of those who accept political pluralism, are not averse to its inharmonious cacophony, and who do not see conflict as something to be overcome. At its best (which is not all the time, clearly) partisanship's moral significance is located here, in the commitment to pluralism and regulated political rivalry. While they try to speak to everyone, partisans do not imagine they speak for everyone. And it takes self-discipline to acknowledge partiality and resist the urge to claim the mantle of the nation, to pretend to represent all "real" Americans. Partisans are not always faithful to this obligation, but representative democracy depends on their acknowledging (as the word "partisan" suggests) that they are only a part and not the whole. It takes discipline to accept that every victory is partial and temporary, only good until the next election.

Every anti-liberal, antidemocratic ideology rejects political pluralism and its incarnation in political parties. We have already pointed out how populism identifies the one "true" people and rejects claims of belonging by others. Authoritarianism insists on a single, sovereign guiding will. Fascism glorifies one *volk*—the rest of the population is a contamination that must be excised for the health of the whole. Nationalism is commonly rooted in a single ethnic and cultural identity. Marxism sees one class, the proletariat, initiating the final emancipatory revolution. For holists of every stripe, political parties are a symptom of abhorrent divisions, and by their avowed partiality to a particular interest, opinion, principle, or ambition—a partiality confirmed by the existence of rival parties—they are abominable. Today's conspiracist mind-set exhibits this loathing, and is antiparty as we will show.

The practice of organized, open competition for power, which can be summarized in the phrase "the legitimate opposition," only began in the nineteenth century. Before that, every effort to overturn the ruling group was a conspiracy, and all conspiracies were by definition seditious. The rise of regulated party rivalry and, with it, the loyal opposition—an opposition that aims to replace the ruling group but does not aim to overturn the whole regime or the constitution—might have made the very concept of political conspiracy obsolete.

Why secretly conspire to overturn those in power when you can organize partisans in the open? Parties bring political conflict out in the open, but in the historical transition from cabal to democratic institution, open partisanship is no tonic for those who loathe political pluralism. For holists of every stripe, the regulated rivalry of parties, the notion of a loyal opposition, and the institution of contested elections are all anathema.

The alarming response today by those who reject the value of conflict and opposition is to delegitimate parties. They do this by once again casting parties as conspiracies. The new conspiracists see themselves as standing for the greatness of the real America and see the opposition party as the enemy. After his first State of the Union address, Donald Trump spoke of Democrats who did not applaud as being un-American, even treasonous. "Can we call that treason?" Trump asked. "Why not? I mean, they certainly didn't seem to love our country very much." He continued, "Even on positive news, really positive news like that, they were like death and un-American," he said, repeating, "un-American. Somebody said treasonous. I mean, yeah, I guess, why not."[8] His press secretary followed up: Democrats need to decide "whether they hate the president more than they love their country."[9]

The Process of Delegitimation

Persistent conspiracist denigration of parties and partisanship has the effect of delegitimating them. The process does not happen all at once. It proceeds piece by piece, slowly enough that one might not perceive what is at stake, especially given background conditions in which Americans have often disparaged parties and partisanship. We isolate three steps by which the new conspiracism takes us beyond virulent partisan antagonism to delegitimation. This is not to suggest that each step takes place in order. The "steps" are conceptual rather than chronological. In fact, they are all being taken simultaneously.

The process starts by delegitimating opposition candidates and party leaders. Birtherism depicted Barack Obama's presidency as a violation of the Constitution, and Trump is the chief birther, who referred to Obama as the "quote 'president.'"[10] He brought the conspiracist accusation from the periphery to the mainstream of political discourse, where it infected the formal processes of elections and threatened to keep Obama's name from appearing on the Kansas ballot in the reelection campaign of 2012. Referring to the accusation that Obama was foreign-born and therefore his name should not appear on the ballot, Kansas secretary of state Kris Kobach said at the time, "I don't think it's a frivolous objection. . . . I do think the factual record could be supplemented."[11] This was as Obama was finishing his first term as president and more than a year after the White House released his long-form birth certificate.

In the 2016 election, the power of conspiracism was harnessed to delegitimate Hillary Clinton's candidacy by representing her as a criminal. Clinton was implicated in a grand scheme to weaken America, a scheme "that encompassed the entire global power structure—the banks, the government, the media, the guardians of secular culture, as well as financial titans including the billionaire investor George Soros, Federal Reserve Chairwoman Janet Yellen, and Goldman Sachs CEO Lloyd Blankfein."[12] There are no commonsense boundaries of plausibility when it comes to Clinton, who was also charged with drug running, murder, and pedophilia. "Lock her up!" is a perfect example of the new conspiracist bare assertion.

Delegitimation continues with an attack on the entire opposition party. The attack does not stop at saying that the opposing party is wrong because it propounds a flawed understanding of the public interest. It entails more than mistrust of the opposition and cynicism about motives. And it is not content to dispense with civility. For example, in connection with the 2018 midterm elections, Trump warned that if Democrats win a majority in Congress they will not only "overturn everything we've done" but do it "violently." He identified the whole party with militant groups like Antifa—"and you look at some of these groups, these are violent people."[13] The opposition is cast as a danger to the nation. This amounts to the delegitimation of a defining element of representative democracy: the idea of the loyal opposition.

Because this step is so important, how the opposition party comes to be cast as illegitimate demands an extended look. The disqualification of parties is sometimes a legal matter, determined by the Constitution itself. In many countries with constitutions written after World War II, there are provisions for banning certain parties. Those provisions are based on the idea that a certain party is opposed to the regime itself (the Nazi Party in Germany, for example), that it betrays the identity of the country, and that it threatens the security of the state. The US Constitution, written before the era of democratic parties, has no clause officially banning certain parties. In the US, delegitimation is carried on in the arena of public opinion. We are now seeing that happen as the new conspiracists bring their charges against the opposition party. And when they do, they exploit the same arguments that might be used to formally disqualify parties in other countries.

One claim is that the opposition party acts unconstitutionally: it abuses authority and passes illegal legislation or executive orders—for example, the charge that Obama is a "lawless president" who, with the acquiescence of partisans in Congress, repeatedly took unilateral and unconstitutional action on gun control, gay rights, the minimum wage, contraception, and climate change.[14] His administration amounted to, it was said, an "eight-year constitutional crisis."[15] To be sure, disagreements about the boundaries of presidential power have fueled partisan contestation from the 1790s to the present. George W. Bush, for example, was said to abuse his authority by appending to legislation signing statements that sometimes contradicted Congress's intent for the law he was reluctantly signing.[16] Questioning the bounds of presidential authority is part of normal politics. But when it extends to saying that virtually everything a president and his party does in office is a willful violation of constitutional constraints, then political contestation slides into delegitimation.

A second delegitimating charge is more elusive: the opposition party conspires to subvert foundational values to a degree that alters national identity. The charge is that the party's covert goal is to deny America as a Christian nation, depreciate America as a white nation, empower "takers and suckers," and cede sovereignty to the "new world order." The claim is simple: an entire group—Muslims, "liberals," Jews, African Americans—harbors ambitions to seize control, and the opposition party uses the electoral process to ally with them to create a rival society, an alien nation. The opposition is said to be nothing less than an existential threat.

Delegitimation nearly always involves a third charge: the opposition is willfully ruinous, treasonous. The party's policy of international aggression, or its failures to act aggressively, are not just ineffective or immoral but in fact designed to weaken the nation militarily and materially. Thus, Democratic partisans are said to be deliberately reducing America's defenses, ignominiously degrading its stature in the world, and giving away its resources. The party is a front directed, dominated, disciplined, and controlled by malicious forces who have made their way into government. The opposition is collaborating with foreign powers or is the pawn of hostile governments. Hillary Clinton "meets in secret with international banks to plot the destruction of U.S. sovereignty."[17] Marco Rubio accused Obama of the same thing—selling out the country to foreign powers: "Let's dispel the fiction that Barack Obama doesn't know what he's doing," Rubio said on the campaign trail. "He knows exactly what he's doing. He's trying to change the country."[18]

The effect is delegitimation. From the conspiracist standpoint, a victory for Democrats is not just a loss for Trump Republicans; it is the result of nefarious dealings, and it is dangerous. As a result, conspiracists cannot accept, as partisans must, that defeat is temporary. For them, there is no question of a cycle of elections bringing parties to power alternately or of parties sharing power. Rather, the opposition must be disabled from effectively occupying office. It must be rendered impotent. That was Steve Bannon's consolation at a moment when he thought Trump could not win the election: "Our back-up strategy is to fuck her [Hillary Clinton] up so bad that she can't govern."[19]

Delegitimation of the opposition party is also carried on by disenfranchising its partisans. Partisan efforts to create structural electoral advantage for themselves have a long history. But voter suppression today is justified in conspiracist terms. The mechanisms of disenfranchisement include creating obstacles to registration, narrowing windows for voting, reducing the availability of polling places, requiring specific forms of identification, and purging voter rolls. These measures are meant to legally disenfranchise voters or to create voter confusion and intimidation. The moves are strategic—to entrench Republican majorities—but the effort is now inseparable from the conspiracist claim that unnamed forces are delivering millions of fraudulent voters to the polls. The putative "problem of voter fraud" is at the heart of Trump's signature conspiracy tale about how he lost the popular vote.

This is delegitimation: representing the opposition candidate as a criminal and the opposition party as a whole as a dangerous enemy to be not only defeated electorally but in fact neutralized. This is not party politics as usual. It is a critical step in the undoing of a democratic system of parties and partisanship.

The culminating step is to impugn *all* political parties. In this view, Democrats are not the only ones with nefarious, concealed aims. Republicans are complicit. They are weak dupes or willful co-conspirators. Both parties own the rigged status quo. They form a duopoly. Conspiracists see collusion between parties equally responsible for marauding immigrants, Muslim terrorists, and the collapse of national sovereignty and identity.

Trump is perfectly cast to preside over this moment. Parties and partisans frustrate him. He is impulsive and would work without and around them, bully them, or disregard them. And no party or partisan is immune from his diffuse conspiracist claims. This third step toward the delegitimation of parties per se—delegitimation of the defining institution of democracy and our system of representation—is now discernible.

What is already in full-blown, Technicolor effect is the delegitimation of a system of representation that embraces political pluralism, a system requiring regulated rivalry, loyal opposition, and the bedrock democratic "agreeing to disagree."

The Contrast: Progressive Antipartyism

The new conspiracist assault on parties feeds off a long history of antipartyism in America. But it has very little in common with the most important antiparty movement, Progressivism, whose wholesale attacks on the party system were justified as a *defense* of democracy. The antiparty charge has historically been made this way in the name of making the system more democratic. In this respect, conspiracist antipartyism is something new; it aims not to improve democracy but rather to delegitimate it.

Progressivism in the late nineteenth century decried parties as "perverters of the democratic spirit."[20] Parties and the interests they served amounted to a system of corruption, collusion, and fraud. Their antidemocratic instruments included party bosses, patronage, spoils, and voters who were not persuaded but bought. (In a twist, the suffragette Charlotte Perkins Gilman described political parties as institutional expressions of "inextricable masculinity" and anticipated that once women were enfranchised, "a flourishing democratic government [could] be carried on without any parties at all.")[21] Progressives connected the dots to reveal patterns of corruption. They called it muckraking. They revealed a conspiratorial combination of corporate monopolies and party bosses.

Their purpose was to wrest power from political machines, and in place of parties Progressives championed what they saw as morally improving institutions. Among them were nonpartisan local government and public commissions that relied on nonpartisan expertise. Acknowledging that political representation and elections might be necessary, Progressives promoted primary elections in which candidates were not identified with a party and voters were independents, not partisans.

Above all, though, Progressives championed direct participatory action over political representation: initiatives and referenda, mechanisms to recall elected officials, constitutional conventions, and experiments in deliberative democracy by ordinary citizens. Progressives could talk about parties as perverters of democracy because they had a theory of democracy.

Conspiracist antipartyism today is not the product of sober confrontation with the limitations of party democracy. Indeed, it is divorced from institutional considerations of representation altogether. Nor do conspiracists uphold a purified image of democracy in which independents replace partisans; their appeal is not to voters who describe themselves as independents and claim to make their decisions about candidates case by case without consideration of the collective partisan "we." The new conspiracism assaults parties and partisanship, but not for the sake of reform; it is wholly negative.

For our part, we think the Progressives went too far in their derogation of parties and partisanship. We don't cede the moral high ground to independents and technocrats. And we do not champion direct participatory democracy. But despite our criticisms of this view, we recognize that Progressive antipartisanship was motivated by a desire to renovate democracy, to elevate it and purify it and make it more legitimate.

Another American political tradition—pragmatism—is also antiparty, and it provides another contrast to conspiracist delegitimation. A perennial feature of American politics is the pragmatic call to "just fix it," or, "How about being realistic and just solving the problem?" From this standpoint, parties seem like needless sources of gridlock, obstacles to getting things done. For his part, Trump valorizes action over discussion. As he says, "The problem with politicians is that [they're] all talk and no action. It's true. All talk, it's all bullshit."[22] And he says, "Only I can fix it." Trump's boast doesn't align with pragmatism any more than it does with Progressivism, though. Pragmatism is a collective process of democratic decision-making. It focuses on specific problems, policies, and outcomes, and it looks to specialized knowledge and expertise. Pragmatism is concrete, specific, and technocratic. The new conspiracist mind-set, in contrast, is intractably unpragmatic, uninterested in the intricacies of decision-making and policy-making. The new conspiracism is not about making democracy or government work at all.

The Partisan Penumbra

We've set out the steps conspiracism takes in delegitimating not this or that partisan or party but the system of political representation, which rests on the principle of regulated party rivalry and commitment to seeing the opposition as a loyal opposition. Still, our conclusion that the new conspiracism is antiparty may be jarring. After all, it is rightly charged to the president and many of his appointed officials, and it has the sometimes implicit, often pronounced, support of Republicans in Congress. The Left has its conspiracists, but they do not yet approach the new conspiracists in number or influence. Above all, the Left is not party to the delegitimizing thrust of the new conspiracism. Given this asymmetry, isn't the new conspiracism itself partisan?

Ultimately, conspiracist delegitimation of parties and partisanship is not restricted to one political actor or one side of an issue, one ideology or one party. But in the more immediate near term, conspiracism is aligned with radical conservatism. This alignment is visible in the effect of the new conspiracism—

the way it assaults government. We call this the new conspiracism's "partisan penumbra."

What explains the alliance of conspiracists and radical conservatives is their mutual hostility to active government, in particular to the complex business of regulation and enforcement located in the administrative state. The administrative state, with its capacity to design and implement complicated, long-term policy, is the legacy of the Progressive Era and the New Deal. Because of this legacy, conservatives have always been wary of it, and radical conservatives opposed to it. The new conspiracism shares and amplifies this opposition. Bannon advocates "deconstruction of the administrative state." The echo is audible in Trump's presidential proclamation: the United States needs "a good 'shutdown.'"[23] The result, in this moment, is congruence between conspiracism and radical conservatism housed in the Republican Party with its slogan, "Government is not the solution to our problems. It is the problem."

In its modest iteration, conservatism sought to correct the alleged excesses of New Deal liberalism. As Ronald Reagan explained, in his youth he shared the goals of Franklin D. Roosevelt and the New Deal, but, as he saw it, the Democratic Party became more extreme. "I didn't leave the Democratic Party," Reagan pronounced. "The party left me." It was also Reagan who gave Republicanism its antigovernment organizing principle. In its current iteration, conservatism seeks to reverse the New Deal legacy altogether. This more radical and destructive impulse was exemplified by Rick Perry when he insisted during the presidential campaign of 2011 that he would eliminate three federal agencies, but could only name two. The specifics do not matter—what matters is that government be dismantled.

Here is how conspiracism's partisan penumbra—its alliance with radical conservatism—works. Antigovernment partisans in office run into a formidable obstacle: in practice, dismantling government programs is unpopular. People expect government to protect them from dangerous products, to monitor the safety of the water and food supply, to assist victims of natural disasters, to ensure access to health care, to regulate markets, to prosecute frauds, and so on. When Republicans campaign, they tout their commitment to fiscal responsibility, and Republican voters may echo the ideology of shrunken government and astringency, but not when it comes to any particular policy.[24] "The typical conservative cycle runs from backlash [against liberal policies] to embrace [hardline conservative positions] to disappointment." In 2017, while controlling all three branches of government, Republicans enacted enormous increases in government spending, "reversing the only major policy victory of the Tea Party insurgents in 2011." The political scientist Matt Grossmann concluded, "The cycle is born of the infeasibility of conservative goals, especially the American right's attempt to reverse the growth of the welfare and administrative state." Radical Republican conservatism is "a reactionary backlash rather than an alternative governing program."[25]

This is the radical conservative predicament: How to destroy the programs and the institutions that implement them, which people like and endorse? The answer is not to destroy them directly, but instead to delegitimate the infrastructure of the administrative state, and that attack is now effectively carried on in conspiracist terms. Trump is not any sort of recognizable Republican, but his actions align with radical conservatism: attacking the integrity and expertise of civil servants in agencies, hollowing out departments, firing scientists, data collectors, lawyers versed in administration and regulation. Conspiracism helps accomplish what conservatives in office cannot by delegitimating the people and institutions that deliver these policies. This alignment expands the market for conspiracism. It does for radical conservatism some of what it cannot do for itself.

In the moment, this allies many Republicans with conspiracism and gives it a partisan penumbra. But this is not to say that the new conspiracists see themselves as bound to the Republican Party or as promoting a partisan program. In the end, the new conspiracism is not a partisan project. The communities of special knowledge that conspiracists delegitimate—the doctors, economists, and engineers who regulate the safety of airplanes or steward the macroeconomy toward low inflation and sustainable growth—do not belong to one side of the partisan divide. They are what is necessary to make government capable and responsive to popular wants and needs. To undermine them is not to damage liberalism or progressivism or the Left or Democrats or errant Republicans but rather to damage democracy.

That said, for the moment the partisan penumbra of the new conspiracism is indisputably conservative and Republican. While the Left is drawn to classic conspiracism, when it comes to the new conspiracism, it is a mistake to imagine symmetry between the Left and the Right.[26] Left conspiracism is not about the delegitimation of democratic institutions. Though it may seem entrenched, the conspiracist alliance with radical conservatism is contingent, and ultimately the new conspiracism will devour its Republican fellow travelers. For conspiracism is a force that is antithetical to any governing philosophy and to any party. It is the acid that dissolves the institutions and processes—the parties, partisanship, and, as we see in chapter 5, the apparatus of knowledge-based policy—that make democracy work.

Weak Parties, Polarized Parties: Conditions for Conspiracist Delegitimation

The outcome of the conspiracist attack on parties is delegitimation. But escalating conspiracist assaults on parties do not arise in a vacuum. Parties are vulnerable targets. The organizational apparatus of both major parties had been weakened so that, by the time of the 2016 election, official party endorsements had little weight, and party leaders had little capacity to prevent a "hostile takeover" of presidential primaries by outsider candidates. In large part, the vulnerability of parties has to do with money. Wealthy individuals and independent groups spend vast sums advertising in support of candidates and issues as they see fit, so that party leaders and organizations no longer control access to campaign funding. They have lost much of their capacity to vet candidates and hold the party together for governing.

Something else has made parties vulnerable to conspiracist attack: political polarization. Democrats and Republicans in office have moved to the liberal and conservative extremes. And whether or not most citizens are more ideologically extreme than they have been (political scientists dispute this point), they are sorting themselves along polarized party lines. The result is a palpable and measurable polarization in politics and even, alarmingly, in social life. In a 2016 Pew Research Center study, majorities in both parties expressed very unfavorable views of the other party and found the other party a source not only of frustration but also of fear and anger. "More than half of Democrats (55%) say the Republican Party makes them 'afraid,' while 49% of Republicans say the same about the Democratic Party." The proportions are higher among partisans who report "high political engagement." "Thermometer ratings" of hot to cold are very low ("frigid") for the other party's candidate. Large percentages of partisans say the people of the opposite party are more closed-minded, immoral, lazy, dishonest, and unintelligent than other Americans.[27] That helps account for a telling statistic: 49 percent of Republicans and 33 percent of Democrats said they would be "displeased" if their child married someone of the other party.[28] Above all, growing numbers see the opposing party as a "threat."[29]

For many partisans, the substantive grounds of division get eclipsed by the blazing fact of division itself. Then there is no place, no appetite, and no gratitude for the moderates and compromisers. Political polarization invites people to see their political opponents as intractable foes. This prepares the way for conspiracist delegitimation, which sees political opponents as enemies, as an existential threat. Weak party organizations and polarization are fertile ground for new conspiracist delegitimation of parties as a foundation of democracy.

The same partisan polarization has weakened knowledge-producing institutions, making them vulnerable to the new conspiracist delegitimation. In chapter 5 we analyze the conspiracist assaults on knowledge, from simple facts to communities of expertise to the free press. Conspiracism attacks not only knowledge but also skepticism: the capacity to recognize that certainty is provisional and the capacity for self-correction. Both are essential for democratic government, both are virtues necessary for democratic citizenship, and both are targets of the new conspiracists.

5

Knowledge

Administrative and intelligence agencies of government, universities and research centers, communities of expertise, and responsible media all create, assess, correct, and improve the universe of knowledge essential to reasoning about politics and policy. Conspiracism assaults knowledge-producing institutions in ways that are both destructive to democracy and personally disorienting, for, ultimately, conspiracists alter what it means to know something: they claim to own reality, and they seek (with growing success) to impose their reality on everyone.

The new conspiracist mind-set blurs the line between misinformation and good information. It stubbornly asserts and reasserts "both demonstrably false claims *and* unsubstantiated beliefs about the world that are contradicted by the best available evidence and expert opinion."[1] The assault on knowledge begins with rejection of particulars but culminates in denial of the standing of institutions that produce information, beginning with government agencies—the intelligence agencies, the Occupational Safety and Health Administration, the Environmental Protection Agency, the Centers for Disease Control and Prevention, the Congressional Budget Office, the National Institutes of Health, scientific advisory boards, bureaus of statistics, government auditors, and bureaucrats in the Internal Revenue Service. It wantonly discredits nongovernmental sources—scientists, social scientists, public health and education professionals, and research universities. It denies standing to public interest groups and media companies that serve as watchdogs of distortion in the flow of information and explanation. "So don't make the mistake of dismissing the assault on the Congressional Budget Office as some kind of technical dispute," the economist Paul Krugman cautions. "It's part of a much bigger struggle, in which what's really at stake is whether ignorance is strength, whether the man in the White House is the sole arbiter of truth."[2]

Trump in fact presents himself as the arbiter of fact. He insisted that the official figure of deaths in Puerto Rico caused by Hurricane Maria in 2018 was wildly inflated, tweeting, "3000 people did not die . . . this was done by the Democrats in order to make me look as bad as possible." The correct number, he claimed, was in the range of "6 to 18."[3] The new conspiracism politicizes the process by which facts are produced and shrouds facts themselves in a conspiracist cloud.

Delegitimation of authoritatively produced facts and conclusions has potentially dire consequences: the cumulative effect of long-standing attacks on vaccination and on policies to reduce greenhouse gas emissions may be fatal. Elected officials who certainly know better go along, as Senator Rand Paul, a physician, did when, confronted with the conspiracist view that the measles vaccine causes autism—a claim contradicted emphatically by the Centers for Disease Control and Prevention and the American Academy of Pediatrics—he equivocated. Responding to a question during a Republican debate in the fall of 2015 about the spurious vaccine-autism link, he answered, "I'm all for vaccines, but I'm also for freedom."[4] The senator understands herd immunity, which requires a high threshold of a community to be vaccinated, he knows that the vaccine-autism link is fraudulent, and he knows that there is no conspiracy to cover up the so-called link. His stand for "freedom" supports the freedom to ignore science and to refuse to comply with regulations protecting public health. The result is that physicians anticipate major outbreaks of preventable diseases. Conspiracism has the capacity to ignite a "disinformation pandemic."[5]

An iconic exchange from January 22, 2017, crystallizes the conspiracist assault on knowledge. On NBC's *Meet the Press*, Chuck Todd asked presidential adviser Kellyanne Conway why the White House press secretary had repeated Donald Trump's demonstrably false claim that the National Park Service had doctored photographs to diminish the size of the crowd at his inauguration. Conway said, "You're saying it's a falsehood. . . . And our press secretary gave alternative facts to that." Todd responded, "Wait a minute, alternative facts? Alternative facts. . . . Look, alternative facts are not facts. They're falsehoods."[6] The conspiracist response is not to try to validate the "alternative fact" but rather to reject facts and deny the authority of institutions that produce them.

Rejecting Simple Facts: Obama's Birth Certificate

The birther conspiracy, which claims that Barack Obama was born in Kenya and was ineligible for the presidency under the requirements of the Constitution, is a prime example of rejection of simple, verifiable facts. The conspiracy was born in 2008, the work of a California dentist, Orly Taitz. Within a year it was afloat—an identifiable bit of malicious flotsam swirling amid the larger current of opposition to Obama. In 2011 Trump became what the *New York Times* called "a nonstop 'birther.'" On Fox News, he implored the president to prove his native birth: "Why doesn't he show his birth certificate?" On NBC, Trump said, "I'm starting to think that he was not born here," and, "He grew up and nobody knew him." Over and over again, Trump asserted that he had sent a team of investigators to Hawaii to unearth information: "They cannot believe what they are finding."[7] Trump amplified the allegation of foreignness by suggesting that Obama was a secret Muslim: "He cannot give a birth certificate. . . . He doesn't have a birth certificate, or, if he does, there's something on that certificate that is very bad for him. . . . Where it says 'religion' it might have 'Muslim.'"[8] (Birth certificates in the United States do not list religion.)

Birtherism, like the new conspiracism generally, takes the form of sheer assertion. Its spread was assisted by the failure of many political leaders to speak truth to conspiracy. Plenty of officials remained silent; plenty of others chimed in. Senator Ted Cruz told supporters, "We need to send Barack Obama back to Chicago. I would like to send him back to Kenya." In 2009 thirteen Republican members of Congress sponsored a bill requiring presidential candidates to include in official papers a copy of their birth certificates—pandering to those who insisted that Obama had failed to produce reliable documentation. A typical Republican response to the birther claim was support without responsibility: "I would love to know more. What I know is troubling enough."[9] In the same way, officials claimed ignorance when asked to provide evidence for Trump's charge that former president Obama had tapped his phones by saying, "That's above my pay grade."[10] When President Obama produced his long-form birth certificate proving that he was born in Honolulu, public belief in birtherism declined overall, polling shows, indicating acceptance of official record keeping. But no documentation could cause hard-core birthers to stop repeating, much less correct, the conspiratorial accusation.[11]

It turns out that conspiracist claims are easy to create, and easy for officials to embellish, endorse, or just allow to play out. What lies behind complicity by insinuation, equivocation, or silence? As we detail in chapter 7, representatives are vulnerable to angry constituents who subscribe to conspiracy. When reelection is in jeopardy, or an official is haunted by the specter of a potential primary challenge, silence or coy encouragement seems a safer posture than correcting the record and offending one's supporters.

Without official equivocation, conspiracism could not spread from the periphery to the mainstream. Mainstream media are more likely to report on these claims when they come from a member of Congress, a governor, or the chairperson of the Republican Party. Silence on the part of leaders contributes to the confusion of citizens, who can think that when elected officials do not rebut birtherism, there must be "something there." Equivocation gives the birther claim an aura of respectability as, at a minimum, a subject that warrants discussion. And it maddens and confounds officials and citizens who accept official evidence of Obama's birthplace, who recognize birtherism as an attempt to delegitimize the first African American president, and who understand that the polarized partisan divide is now epistemic as well as political. Conspiracism creates a schism over what it means to know something.

Most officials who stand aside in silence, or who, like Cruz, subtly encourage the conspiracy, are cynically, politically self-protective. They enable the conspiracy, but what really fuels it and keeps it burning are those of a different cast who themselves possess the conspiracist mind-set—like Trump. Obama released his birth certificate in 2008, and his long-form birth certificate in 2012. Even after that, Trump tweeted that "an extremely credible source" called him to tell him the long-form certificate was a fraud.[12] Trump doubled down on the birther conspiracy in 2013, when the health director of Hawaii was killed in a plane accident: "How amazing, the State Health Director who verified copies of Obama's 'birth certificate' died in plane crash today. All others lived."[13] It was only when he came under severe questioning in September 2016, after receiving the Republican presidential nomination, that Trump grudgingly conceded that Obama was born in the United States. Even then, he did something astonishing—he attributed the origin of the birther claim to Hillary Clinton.[14] This impulsive add-on conspiracy reveals that the new conspiracism is not about making sense of a confusing world but rather about tribal identity and tribal enmity.

Birtherism epitomizes intransigent denial of simple facts. Denial does not stop with unjustified rejection of the records of ordinary civil servants working in the Hawaii state government, however. Nor are simple facts the only thing at stake. Knowledge is less a repository of settled facts than it is a process by which we come to understand the world. This process has integrity when it is disciplined and unbiased—as scientists or professionals in the news media try to be. The new conspiracist assault is expansive, and it ultimately takes aim at knowledge-producing institutions wholesale. Consider the dangerous assault on the science of climate change.

The Assault on Expert Knowledge: Climate Change

The attack on climate science comes from two sources: self-interested corporations like Exxon, together with their partisan defenders in the Republican Party, and new conspiracists peddling the notion that climate change is a hoax. The first takes the form of an intense but otherwise conventional political attack charging that climate scientists are biased. It claims that scientists have corrupted the integrity of their research because of their partisan leanings or precommitment to a set of conclusions about global warming and its regulatory solutions. The new conspiracists' climate-change hoax attack is, by contrast, more fundamental and ultimately more corrosive because it is invulnerable to refutation and correction. When climate change is characterized as a hoax, the charge is not that climate scientists fail to respect the norms of scientific research or that they fail to submit their findings to peer review or that the science is ideologically biased. Climate conspiracists reject the whole of climate science findings with a bare assertion: "Hoax." They disseminate it and repeat it until it makes a regular appearance in public life and becomes plausible, at least to some.

The infamous unalloyed conspiracist claim is Senator James Inhofe's: "With all the hysteria, all the fear, all the phony science, could it be that manmade global warming is the greatest hoax ever perpetrated on the American people?"[15] Trump calls it a "Chinese hoax" and serves it up with conspiratorial intent: "The concept of global warming was created by and for the Chinese in order to make United States manufacturing noncompetitive."[16] Conspiracist claims are ongoing: we are treated to the assertion that the idea of climate change is spread by environmental groups acting as foreign agents.[17] The president's

account of the ruse now extends to a global conspiracy of scientists themselves, and he justifies his ongoing climate denial
with "people are saying." After Trump told CBS reporter Lesley Stahl, "They say that we had hurricanes that were far
worse than what we just had with Michael," Stahl pushed back,
"Who says that? 'They say?'" In response, Trump simply repeated his mantra: "People say. People say that . . ."[18]

Oil companies and Republican officials who charge climate
scientists with bias make arguments that can be refuted by
showing that the science is *not* biased. Accusations of bad faith
and bias, of distortion and misinformation, are an ugly politics
to be sure; it is certainly not politics according to the deliberative ideal in which reasons are met with reasons in a common
effort to justify public policy in the most convincing way. But
it is a politics in which it is possible for intentional misinformation to be countered by better information. In contrast to
the corporate misinformation campaign, the new conspiracist
"hoax" deniers serve up not misinformation but fabulation.

The corporate attack on climate science is tangled and secretive, so that ferreting out and exposing these machinations
has been difficult. Nevertheless, the charge of corporate conspiracy has proved to be warranted. Exxon (which in 1998
merged with Mobil to form ExxonMobil) modeled its deception on the original strategy of the tobacco industry: a system-
atic effort of a small group of corporate-funded scientists to
counter medical findings that smoking was a cause of cancer.[19]
Employing some of the same scientists, the fossil fuel industry
funded so-called experts to cast doubt on global warming. Earlier, Exxon had itself done state-of-the-art climate research,
but the company reversed itself in 1988 when legislative efforts
to address climate change by regulating carbon emissions were

gathering force. In an attempt to influence public opinion and to change the terms of the legislative debate, Exxon began to support denial groups and make demonstrably false claims: the company head stated in 1997, "The earth is cooler today than it was twenty years ago."[20]

ExxonMobil and its corporate cousins in the fossil fuel industry have concrete interests to defend: they fear "stranded assets"—oil and gas in the ground that would be unmarketable or less valuable if limits were imposed on fossil fuel production. In service to profitability, they have tried to shape public policy by distorting the public's understanding of the threat posed by climate change. They are engaged in an intentional misinformation campaign. They understand the scientific consensus but are trying to obscure it. They do not have a compromised relation to reality; they are corrupt.

And in their misinformation campaign, they claim the authority of science for themselves. Coteries of billionaires and conservative activists have created their own institutes, publishing outlets, and lobbying operations to demote what they represent as the liberal hegemony in research and policy. They do this by producing alternative facts. A 2013 study of climate-change denial publications shows that 83 percent of them have ties to conservative think tanks—the Cato Institute, the Heartland Institute, the Competitive Enterprise Institute, the Hoover Institution, and others.[21]

While the corporate misinformation campaign accepts the idea of expertise in principle—and even produces its own pseudoexperts to rival scientific experts—the new conspiracist climate-change denial represents a more complete rejection of expertise. The goal of climate-change hoaxers is not to persuade legislators and regulators; it is not programmatic.

For those who claim climate change is a hoax, climate science is just one target in the sweeping attack on the authority of specialized knowledge. Expertise as such is disdained.

So we now have a potent brew: the conspiracist mind-set broadcasting that climate change is a hoax aimed at weakening America, wrapped up with a cynical design by fossil fuel corporations and their political allies to undermine facts in order to protect their financial interests. The conspiracist deniers allow the corporate deniers to become more extreme and even more closed to the normal terms of political discussion and negotiation. Conspiracism pushes Republican officials into acquiescing in the idea of a climate-change hoax, even if they do not affirm it. Instead, they equivocate and resort to the mantra "I am not a scientist." Flirtation with wholesale climate-change denial makes it easier for them to reject any policy to address global warming. It has allowed dark money to have a more extreme effect. As conservative political consultant Karl Rove said to oil executives in Dallas, "People call us a vast right-wing conspiracy, but we're really a half-assed right-wing conspiracy. Now it's time to get serious."[22] They did.

Up until 2010, it was common for Republican candidates to run on a "green energy" platform, even to support cap-and-trade policies as a way to mitigate carbon emissions. But after the Supreme Court *Citizens United* decision liberated corporate money in political campaigns, things changed. Charles and David Koch, who own 84 percent of the oil refining company Koch Industries, poured money into a campaign to pressure Republicans into opposing any action on global warming. Their strategy worked: "Republicans who asserted support for climate change legislation or the seriousness of the climate threat saw their money dry up or faced a primary challenger." By 2017, when Trump initiated US withdrawal from the Paris

Agreement on climate change, every member of the elected Republican leadership united in praise of the drastic move.[23]

Taken together, conspiracist hoax claims and the corporate misinformation and campaign funding strategy suppress the realities of climate change and distort public discussion in remarkable ways. For example, they have resulted in a gag rule that prevents the military from taking facts about climate change into account in its planning. A 2003 Pentagon report recognized rising sea levels and desertification as security threats, and a 2014 Department of Defense report "categorized climate conflict as a *near term* strategic challenge." Yet 216 members of Congress supported an amendment blocking the military from considering the impact of climate change in its strategic planning.[24] In another case, the word *climate* was eliminated from the mission statement of the National Oceanic and Atmospheric Administration.[25] Across the board, offices and programs with responsibility for collecting and analyzing data are eliminated or starved of resources; the Trump administration Environmental Protection Agency announced its intention to defund satellites and ocean buoys that keep track of climate changes. As environmental activist Bill McKibben wrote, "We're not just going to ignore the mounting evidence, we're going to stop collecting it."[26] Government scientists and other professionals responsible for estimating the risks of climate change are not the only ones whose work is obstructed and who face this malignant normality; on a vast swath of issues affecting public health and security, whole agencies are going dark.

The nexus of assaults on climate science advances the incremental corrosion of specialized knowledge. It severely inhibits government from guarding against the global danger of the extinction of species and destruction of human habitats.

Conspiracism may abet a particular set of corporate interests today, but arrant denigration of factuality, scientific research, and expertise degrades government decision-making. It is undermining not only one particular set of policies on one issue—climate change—but every policy and every program.

Fake News

We have seen how the new conspiracism rejects facts, as in the birther story, and how it denigrates expertise, as in the climate-change hoax conspiracy. Its assault extends further to denying standing to the institutions that produce knowledge—most notably, today, the free press. Everyone can see that Trump and other politicians attack the press. What is less appreciated is that this is an element in the broader new conspiracist phenomenon.

Politics is frequently a scene of baseless and defamatory accusations and strategic lies, but as used today, the charge "fake news" is something new.[27] It goes beyond the claim of a deliberate misinformation campaign, of misleading reports and malicious fakery.[28] The charge is not simply a label applied to news coverage that is erroneous or deceptive or biased. Fake news is an accusation of conspiracy. It is meant to convey that the mainstream news media are secretly colluding to defeat Trump and to disempower his supporters.

For example, Trump adopted a claim from the conspiracist website Infowars ("Scandal: Mass Media Whitewashes Islamic Terror in Berlin") that the media were deliberately refusing to report terrorist attacks. "It's gotten to a point where it's not even being reported," Trump asserted, during (of all things) a talk to military leaders at Central Command. "And in many cases the very, very dishonest press doesn't want to report it.

They have their reasons, and you understand that."[29] "Fake news" as a conspiracist charge has become a part of everyday politics: in the first year of his presidency, Trump tweeted about fake news 180 times.[30] He is not alone in seeing the media itself as a conspiracy. A host of conservative broadcasters demonize the mainstream press, labeling the *New York Times*, the *Washington Post*, CNN, and other outlets "drive-bys," as in drive-by killers.[31] In fact, the very term *mainstream* has become a term of abuse: it is a red line, demarking a category of journalism that is beyond the pale.

DONALD J. TRUMP ✔@REALDONALDTRUMP
FAKE NEWS media knowingly doesn't tell the truth. A great danger to our country. The failing @nytimes has become a joke. Likewise @CNN. Sad!
10:09 PM—24 Feb 2017
25,62425,624 Retweets 103,893103,893 likes[32]

Fake news conspiracism is not a theory—it is a rallying cry. The mainstream media in Trump's characterization is "the opposition party"[33] and, worse, the "enemy of the people."[34] Here, too, rage and repetition are key to delegitimation: "I'm making this presentation directly to the American people. . . . The press, honestly, is out of control. . . . I watch CNN. It's so much anger and hatred. . . . The public gets it. . . . They start screaming at CNN." The next day the president tweeted, "The FAKE NEWS media (failing@nytimes, @NBCNews, @ABC, @CBS, @CNN) is not my enemy. It is the enemy of the American People."[35] At a South Carolina rally, he singled out the reporters covering his event: "These people back here are the worst. . . . They are so dishonest. . . . Absolute scum. Remember that. Scum. Scum. Totally dishonest people."[36] At a subsequent rally, Trump again raised the specter of violence, proclaiming that he would not execute reporters: "I hate some of these people, I hate 'em," Trump said. "But I would never kill them. . . . Uh, let's see, uh. . . . No, I would never do that."[37]

We quote Trump's words at length in order to emphasize that the charge of fake news diverges from the way in which politicians regularly vilify the media. Think of Richard Nixon: "The press is the enemy," he said, "because they're trying to stick the knife right in our groin."[38] Nixon was speaking privately to his closest advisers; Trump is pugnaciously vilifying the press as a public enemy in public. His aim is to destroy the legitimacy of the press as an independent source of knowledge by representing it as an organized conspiracy.

It bears saying that reporting is an irreplaceable resource for government accountability. The press provides the forum where public figures and citizens bear witness to events. There is no substitute for the service that a free press renders to democracy—a press corps that sees it as a professional responsibility to engage in a process of employing reliable sources to render an account of events that is as accurate as possible. The point of incessant charges of "fake news" is to deny standing to the press not with the comparatively benign portrait of an institution that does not care about getting things right but with the dark portrait of an institution with nefarious reasons for misleading the public. The conspiracist substitute for the standards that constitute journalistic integrity is, as we have said, repetition and the affirmation of unsupported claims. Consider this exchange between the president and conservative news anchor Bill O'Reilly. Asked whether there is any validity to reports that Trump is unable to back up his claim that three million illegal alien votes cost him the popular vote, the president replied by invoking the only source of validation that mattered: "Many people have come out and said I'm right."[39]

These conspiracist charges have an impact. "Nearly all Republicans and Republican-leaning independents (92%) think that traditional news outlets report false or misleading stories at least sometimes," and "more than two-thirds (65%) say fake news is usually reported because 'people have an agenda.'"[40] The comprehensive way in which conspiracism denies standing to the press has now raised alarm even among conservatives who recognize that they went too far in the past in their attacks on the press. Charles Sykes, a conservative radio talk show host, took stock: his audience "has been conditioned to reject reporting from news sites outside of the conservative media ecosystem." The price, he said, "turned out to be far higher than [he] imagined." He continued, "The cumulative effect of the attacks was to delegitimize these outlets and essentially destroy much of the right's immunity to false information. We thought we were creating a savvier, more skeptical audience. Instead, we opened the door for President Trump, who found an audience that could be easily misled."[41]

The Assault on Skepticism

What we've discussed—the assault on simple fact, expert knowledge, and the press—is no secret today. *Do Facts Matter?*, asks the title of a recent book by two political scientists, and the implication of the question is that the place of elemental facts in public decision-making has been eroded.[42] This account and others like it attribute the erosion in large part to political polarization and back-and-forth charges of partisan bias. Since the start of mass survey research, political scientists have learned how partisan bias forms a perceptual screen that distorts people's view of the world. So does motivated reasoning and confirmation bias, which we discussed in chapter 2. All this is problematic for democratic politics, but it can be defended against. Its worst distortions are corrigible. In principle, political polarization can abate, bias can be disclosed, and facticity can be restored.

Our point in this chapter is that the new conspiracist invention of reality introduces a different assault on knowledge. Its fabulations sever the connection between assertions and beliefs on the one hand and anything verifiable in the world on the other. This immunizes conspiracist claims from scrutiny and doubt. What follows is that the new conspiracists undercut not only knowledge but also skepticism. This matters, first, because the assault on skepticism is damaging to democracy. It is also important to refute those scholars of conspiracism who represent it as an adventurous exercise in critical thinking and radical doubt.

A romantic characterization has it that conspiracism is a skeptical disposition. Conspiracism, the argument goes, "disrupt[s] complacent, consensual, transparent theories of politics" and involves us "in a reiterative back-and-forth that mobilizes doubt and reassurance. . . . The narrative pivot . . . involves the step away from belief and into skepticism."[43] Conspiracy entrepreneurs encourage this description. They adopt the label of critical thinkers for themselves. When the responsible media attempt to negate conspiracist narratives like Pizzagate, conspiracists accept the challenge. They characterize mainstream factual accounts as evidence of the media's participation in the conspiracy.[44] In addition, they exploit mainstream refutations as an occasion for asking, "Who do you trust?" They rebut the charge that they are fantastic propagators of "fake news" directly. On the contrary, they argue, *they* are the critical thinkers. As they see it, their alternative sites are teaching information consumers to be skeptical, to see themselves as "citizen journalists," to get all the facts and make up their own minds. (As did the armed conspiracist who turned up at the pizzeria in Washington, DC, ready to "self-investigate" the alleged child sex ring.)[45]

In fact, the new conspiracism is the enemy of skepticism, of intellectual humility and openness to the possibility of error and correction. As we've seen, its proponents deny the standing of knowledge-producing institutions and reject simple facts, expert judgment, and the reliability of researchers and journalists. They reject the resources necessary for testing their assumptions. Their certainty is at odds with skepticism; they are without residual doubt that things are as they represent them. So the new conspiracism doubles down: it corrodes both knowledge and skepticism.

Knowledge-producing institutions are essential to democracy; so is skepticism. Experts should not be deferred to simply because of their bona fides—their degrees or their status. Nor should the authority of knowledge-producing institutions such as the free press, the scientific community, or data- and analysis-oriented governmental agencies be accepted without question. Experts are sometimes wrong, science incomplete, and facts, theories, and explanations inaccurate—even absent corruption and bad intentions. Orthodox approaches can stifle new and better ones, and the normative assumptions and judgments behind expert claims can be hidden.

We are aware that the processes that generate knowledge are such that what we think we know can be wrong. The processes sometimes produce failures. Think of security agencies' intelligence about weapons of mass destruction in Iraq or the deregulation of financial institutions in the 1980s and 1990s.

Our best "intelligence" may be wrong; the best economists may be wrong. Beyond error, there is the possibility of corruption. Officials and sometimes entire agencies of government can turn against the people they are meant to serve, like the federal and state agencies whose bad science and cover-ups hid the egregious political decisions that allowed the public water supply in Flint, Michigan, to be contaminated with high levels of lead.[46] The result was large-scale environmental injustice, and this violation of the public trust is not an isolated one.

There are good reasons, then, for democratic citizens to withhold deference, to raise questions about experts, and to hold them accountable for their judgments. This is wholesome skepticism. Conspiracism is not skepticism. In its indiscriminate denial of standing to knowledge-producing institutions, it undercuts the basis for criticism: a commitment to evidence, impartial analysis, and ongoing research. And conspiracism undercuts the habits of doubt that empower us to question and test how we know what we think we know.

Specialized knowledge is essential to democracy, but we acknowledge that it is also a challenge to democracy because it raises the specter of rule by experts—what philosopher Jürgen Habermas called technocracy. Our defense of knowledge-producing institutions does not imply the view that those who produce knowledge have authoritative understanding of how it should be deployed in the political world. Often what is at issue is not the scientific or philosophic truth of things as judged by the internal standards of the expert community but rather their significance and weight for the purposes of politics.[47] What facts, arguments, and conclusions justify or condemn a decision is a matter of political judgment. That is why skepticism requires bridging the world of expertise and democratic politics, and it is most effective when institutions are designed to give it a place in decision-making. Toward this end, democratic theorists and public officials who champion citizen participation have imagined, designed, and experimented with venues for decision-making like "citizen juries," "mini publics," and "deliberative polls," where moderators guide discussion between experts and citizen-deciders. The political theorist Zeynep Pamuk has proposed a "science court" where citizens would question experts directly, demand clarification, probe normative assumptions, and interrogate the strength of evidence and certainty of findings and their implications.[48]

Albert Einstein captured the essential difference between epistemic authority and political authority in his caution about the role of expertise in democracy: "Into the village square we must carry the facts of atomic energy. . . . The nuclear age directly concerns every person in the civilized world. . . . Choices about survival depend ultimately on decisions made in the village square."[49] His point is not that citizens should be participants in nuclear physics research but rather that the use of the technology—the annihilating weapon physicists created—is properly a democratic decision. The same caution applies to the place of expertise in ordinary as well as extraordinary matters.

Skepticism and knowledge-producing institutions go together, and the conspiracist attack on knowledge is also an attack on skepticism. Knowledge does not demand certainty; it demands doubt. Even when we are persuaded that, all things considered, the available evidence and argument point in a certain direction, even after we have resolved to go in that direction, we should be alive to the possibility that in spite of our best effort to get it right, we got it wrong. Our assurance of being right relies on doubt and an iterative process of questioning. And a plurality of knowledge-producing institutions is skepticism's resource. The wealth of specialized knowledge, of science and social science and ethical perspectives, provides platforms from which we consider when experts are wrong, when science is incomplete, when our best understanding of facts and theories and explanations is limited or flawed, and when reasons match or don't match the values we bring to politics. Conspiracists embrace the self-conception that they are skeptics and critical thinkers. But their own epistemic closure undercuts the capacity for skepticism. When knowledge-based pluralism is closed down, when sources are delegitimized and thrust outside the orbit of consideration, when conspiracist transmitters have lost the capacity for receiving, the framework of questioning and assurance is undone.

Degrading Democracy

Three degradations of democracy are the predictable result of the new conspiracist rejection of simple facts, knowledge-producing institutions, and a free press. First, absent common ground, without the possibility of a shared set of facts, standards of verification, and modes of argument, the reasons underlying decisions become illegible. Policy-making is always messy and often a matter of "muddling through," but conspiracism makes it even more chaotic and difficult to hold to account. Misinformation, falsehood, and sheer fabulation seep in. The terrain of politics becomes quicksand. There is no mechanism for self-correction. This is a caution to officials who are politically self-serving fellow travelers in these assaults on knowledge: the conspiracist story "can be an effective political tactic. Believing your own alternative facts, however, is usually not so smart."[50]

A second consequence of conspiracist assaults on knowledge is to prepare the ground for popular acceptance of extreme actions by conspiracists in power. A conspiracist vision of terrorism and a plot to impose sharia law is presented as justification for banning Muslim immigrants and incites private citizens to intimidation and violence against Muslim Americans. A conspiracist vision of "carnage" in inner cities prepares the way for denouncing constraints on law enforcement and encouraging rough behavior by police. A conspiracist claim that the election is rigged is justification for more and more measures of voter suppression. Calling the Justice Department's investigation into Russian interference in the election a prospective coup d'état clears the way for foreign governments to make more aggressive efforts to subvert American elections. This dynamic operates internationally. Trump's daily repetition of the charge "fake news" has become "a cudgel for strongmen," providing a license to autocrats and dictators to escalate their own attacks on journalists.[51]

Conspiracism delivers a third assault: the disorientation that results from the steady barrage of its fabulist claims. We know from experience that the relentless challenge to our sense of reality—to our common sense—is baffling and dispiriting. Looked at more closely, we can understand that it is a special kind of attack on what it means to know something. Conspiracists, including the president, claim to own reality and to impose this reality on the nation.

6

Who Owns Reality?

When political parties are delegitimized, this defining institution of democracy cannot do its work of shaping elections, representation, and the terms of political contestation. When knowledge-producing institutions are delegitimized, they cannot do their work of creating, assessing, and correcting the universe of facts and arguments we need to make decisions about politics and policy.

Yet conspiracism's destructive drive is not reducible to the delegitimation of political parties and of facts, experts, and knowledge-producing institutions, grave as this is. Something else is going on when the new conspiracists are at the helm and have free rein in politics. This "something else" is disorientation, and here we explain the radical disorientation most people feel when confronted with a steady stream of ungrounded conspiracist claims. Closed to the world of shared understanding, conspiracism distorts what it means to know something. At a deeper level, the new conspiracists claim to own reality, and in doing so, they assault our common sense of reality. We experience a special form of anxiety and disorientation. We have been unwillingly drafted into a contest over who owns reality.

The conspiracist in chief has the mind-set and the institutional levers to create his own reality and impose it on the nation. When conspiracists are in a position to impose their compromised sense of reality on us, they do not only produce an account of what is happening that deviates from and often inverts our understanding of the world. They also thrust us toward what we think of as the end of democratic politics, for without a shared understanding of what it means to know something and to hold a common account of the essential contours of political reality, collective political action is impossible. Common sense is the required touchstone of democratic public life, and it is under attack.

Whom Do You Trust?

Conspiracist fabulations have a disorienting effect on many who encounter them. What is responsible for this is the renunciation of the shared realm of facts and experience, which leaves them untethered to the world. Put simply, conspiracism pays no fealty to the common world. We have noted the self-sealing quality and resistance to contrary facts and arguments that characterize conspiracists, as well as the way they communicate their own understanding of things in the form of bare assertion. The new conspiracism is monologic, not dialogic. Or, in other terms, the new conspiracists are transmitters, not receivers.

When we say that the new conspiracists simply assert things and expect others to affirm and repeat them, without evidence or connection to anything verifiable, we do not mean to posit a crude epistemology in which true beliefs are based only on observations that we directly collect and investigations that we directly conduct. Much of what we know, or think we know, we take on trust.

We "know" that vaccines do not cause autism in part because we trust the scientists at the Centers for Disease Control and Prevention who, based on research, attest that this is the case. We "know" that natural selection explains the diversity of species even though we have never studied the fossil record personally because we acknowledge the authority of paleontologists who subject their conjectures to the scrutiny of others through a process of publicizing findings, testing and refining them, and opening themselves to the possibility of refutation. This of course is the process that goes by the popular name "the scientific method." Little of our knowledge depends on direct access to the relevant data or on investigations we carry out ourselves or on direct personal experience. We rely on others.

The fiduciary basis of knowledge makes us vulnerable; if the community in which we place our trust gets it wrong or is corrupt, then what we take to be knowledge may be unjustified and erroneous. Some put their trust in a community of scientists and public health officials who affirm that vaccines do not cause autism; others put their trust in an internet community of anonymous conspiracists who affirm that Hillary Clinton's campaign chairman is running an international child sex-trafficking ring out of a pizzeria. What is the difference?

At the level of the individual who gets his or her knowledge from others, there is not much difference. The difference is found at another level, in the characteristics that define the community whose authority we accept on trust. In one case, these communities are defined by their commitment to publicize the evidence on which their conclusions are based, and thus to subject them to the scrutiny of others. In the other case, the community is defined by access to private knowledge that is unsharable, and by tribal loyalty. The community propagating Pizzagate is defined by the secret key that allowed it to decipher the meaning of Podesta's emails, and by its irrepressible loathing of Hillary Clinton.

When we decide what community is worthy of epistemic trust, we are implicitly also deciding what it means to know something. Reflecting on Donald Trump's historical mishmash of a statement that Andrew Jackson was angry about the Civil War (which began sixteen years after Jackson's death), George Will dissected the president's words to underscore the essential character of his thought. It is not that Trump suffers the disability of an untrained mind tied to "stratospheric self-confidence," Will wrote, or that he is intellectually slothful and misinformed or totally ignorant of ordinary matters of history and of the fact that he has no knowledge of that about which he speaks, or that he is indifferent to being bereft of information. It is not that he is cognitively impaired. "The problem isn't that he does not know this or that, or that he does not know that he does not know this or that. Rather, the dangerous thing is that he does not know what it is to know something." This is dangerous in a president, Will observes, for it "leaves him susceptible to being blown about by gusts of factoids that cling like lint to a disorderly mind."[1] And when that mind demands that its reality be accepted as how things are, we are embattled by an assault on our sense of what it means to know something.

Common Sense

Democracy sometimes depends on trust in communities of special knowledge because it is impossible for every person to work up a scientifically grounded understanding of every domain of expertise that is relevant to politics (and everything else in life). Politics is not all about expertise, though. It is also about what we know from experience. It is about our understanding of what is plausible and implausible in the world of intractable facts. And it is about widely shared judgments that form the moral horizon line for a community. One does not need an expert ethicist to know that torture is inhumane in the extreme, for instance. Nor does one need an expert psychologist to know that separating young refugee children from their parents is traumatic. The shared world of facticity and moral judgment is what we think of as common sense, "that part of our mind and that portion of inherited wisdom," writes political theorist Hannah Arendt, "which all men have in common in any civilization."[2]

Conspiracist claims often defy common sense in its colloquial meaning: they seem absurd to those who do not believe them. Take the claim that the US government helped plan the 9/11 attacks. Why would the government (and who in the government?) attack its own citizens and its own Defense Department? Or, to take the Jade Helm conspiracy of 2015, what motive would drive the US Army to invade the state of Texas, disarm the population, and declare martial law? The weight of political history and absence of any plausible reason put the conspiracist charge outside the bounds of common sense.

Common sense points to things everyone can be assumed to know. Some philosophic accounts of common sense see it as an innate moral sense or an instinctive understanding or a truth about the world that has the consent of all mankind.[3] That is not what we are proposing here. Other invocations of common sense see it as a mark of the reasonableness of some practical measure, as Thomas Friedman does when he invokes common sense as a counterweight to the conspiracist charge that gun control advocates are plotting to overturn the Second Amendment and "take everyone's gun away." As he says, "They know full well that a commonsense banning of all military assault weapons, high-capacity magazines and bump stocks, or mandating universal background checks for gun buyers or to prevent terrorists and the mentally ill from buying guns, would not curb the constitutional right to bear arms."[4] Characterizing something as a matter of common sense points, rhetorically, to the ground to which people can be rallied in agreement that a contrary claim is "beyond the pale."

On our understanding, common sense refers to our acceptance of the intractable facts about the world and our already existing shared experience and understanding about our social world. That is what conspiracism betrays. We need these two elements—facticity and common interpretation—for any collective action in democracy. Political discussion is only possible when we have a stock of shared understandings—this is what common sense supplies. If such and such is a matter of common sense, it is ordinarily not something that can only be appreciated by experts or by particular groups or tribes.

Conspiracism destroys the inclusiveness of the "common" by privileging part of the people—always just a few, who affirm a particular view of reality that is dominated by the unclear but present danger coming from enemies within. True, the new conspiracists appeal to the assent of others—that is exactly the force of the Trumpian phrase "a lot of people are saying."[5] On its face, one might think that appeal to "a lot of people" is an appeal to what everyone can see and understand. That is its rhetorical power—it pretends to comply with exactly the thing it betrays, common sense. When the new conspiracists support the charge of a rigged election by claiming "a lot of people are saying," they are not appealing to what everyone can see, however. On the contrary, "people are saying" entails a dynamic of exclusion by singling out those who "get it," who grasp the true, unrevealed state of affairs. These knowers constitute a co-gnoscenti who affirm one another's divergent sense of reality. "People are saying" is a wink to those who belong to the inner circle. It assigns authority to certify reality to a set of people "like us." Conspiracism departs from the world in which "our lives, thoughts, and public discourse are invisibly restrained by the commonplace, shared assumptions that pass for common sense."[6]

Common sense refers to shared perceptions, experiences, and moral sensibilities, which make democracy possible. Because we share them, we can reflect on them and refer to them in our arguments and assessments and political decisions. Common sense creates a world in which it is possible for people to exchange reasons and feelings that "make sense" to one another—even under conditions of diversity and political conflict. Common sense is a resource against the tyranny that imposes its own reality. This is why Arendt called common sense "the political sense par excellence."[7]

Arendt wrote fiercely about what she called the "sensus communis" against the background of the loss of common sense inflicted by twentieth-century totalitarianism. The "horrible originality" of totalitarianism "exploded our categories of political thought and our standards for moral judgment," she wrote. Totalitarianism is our common touchstone of a regime using terror, propaganda, conspiracy theory, and organized violence to control and reshape not only political behavior but also how people think and what they think, sublimating or even erasing what they used to know. It epitomizes a regime that claims to own reality and creates its own malignant normality, which ordinary people are obliged to live within. As Arendt observed about the effects of totalitarianism, "The growth of meaninglessness has been accompanied by loss of common sense."[8]

We invoke Arendt's reflections not to say that the new conspiracism is like totalitarianism or aspires to it. The twenty-first century has brought its own dangers. We invoke Arendt to underscore conspiracism's destructiveness. And to underscore that, new century though it is, common sense is still the ground of democratic politics. Common sense is the political sense par excellence, Arendt advised, because the capacity for political action and common sense entail each other. When that connection is broken, politics comes to an end. Without recourse to the sometimes unspoken shared understanding of social and political reality embodied in common sense, the scope for collective political action closes down. It is closed down by disorientation. It is closed down by the fact that a new schism has opened up and taken over.

A Different Kind of Polarization

Conspiracism has created a schism more profound and corrosive than the partisan polarization that has beset American politics in recent years. This epistemic polarization has special force. It creates divergent accounts of political reality. It amplifies disorientation. And it has the capacity to reshape our relations to others.

We are talking about a condition in which some inhabit a world where their common sense tells them that it is absurd to suppose Hillary Clinton's campaign chairman is running an international child sex ring from a pizzeria in northwest Washington, DC, and others inhabit a world where that is plausible. There is no conversation that can build a translation bridge connecting this epistemic divide; conspiracism fractures the common political world.

Where the new conspiracism extinguishes common sense, there can be no argument or negotiation or compromise—all of which require some shared terrain of facts and a shared horizon of what it means to know something.

What makes this especially disturbing is that epistemic polarization reaches "all the way down," producing, as we said, polarization at the deep level of mind—distorting what it means to know something. The new conspiracist polarization pursues us all the way down in another respect: it extends from the public sphere and the internet and media into the relations that shape our everyday lives. In this way conspiracism distorts a whole range of social and personal interactions.

Here is what we mean. As conspiracist narratives enter our workplaces and relations with family and neighbors, they eclipse the distinctive characters and experiences of these different domains. Conspiracism distorts our experience of these domains in a uniquely troubling way. We know that the separate spheres of life—the workplace, voluntary associations, informal social groups, the intimate sphere of family and friends—are characterized by different sets of norms and expectations. And we relate to one another differently when we relate as citizens, neighbors, or members of a religious congregation. We have many-sided personalities, and we flourish when we can make moral use of pluralism. A pluralism of separate spheres and shifting involvements among them—that is the personal meaning and value of living in a free civil society. Conspiracism produces epistemic polarization, which can overwhelm the distinct norms and expectations that define these separate spheres and that shape our experiences there. Our way of relating to others in voluntary associations or neighborhoods or workplaces is flattened out. The atmosphere is charged. We begin to ask just one question about others, a question that comes to us from the political sphere but is not the usual political query: not, Do they share my politics? or, Do they agree with me about how to vote? but rather, Do we inhabit the same reality?

We are by now accustomed to partisan polarization. Since the 2016 campaign, it has intensified; people who might not have thought about how friends or neighbors voted in the election now cared intensely. The vote for president became a source of alienation of affection and strained or severed relations. Coworkers, neighbors, and family members who supported the opposition were now viewed as alien, even as demented. People went to psychiatrists about their ruptured friendships and sleepless nights, and psychiatrists went to their psychiatrists. We've experienced this for ourselves or heard or read reports like this one: "I feel like I've been living with a lot of people wearing masks, who have been hiding their true selves, and now, with this vote, their true selves are more apparent."[9]

Similarly, many people have experienced epistemic polarization firsthand and close by. For those who think there is no evidence to show that Hillary Clinton is given to violent criminality, to learn that a friend thinks she ran a pedophile operation would alter the relationship, if not destroy it. There is no common ground on which a conspiracist and a disbeliever can stand to argue about the matter. To discover that a friend subscribes to the QAnon conspiracy, to which we turn shortly, is to see an abyss open up between you.

Conspiracism produces a more disorienting schism than partisan polarization because it affects both political values and identity and basic perceptions of the world. And these are difficult to cabin or contain; totalizing, conspiracism begins to infect domains outside politics. Disorientation is accompanied by anxiety when we witness conspiracists in power attempting to impose their reality on us. Conspiracist-minded officials and their followers are caught up in fabulations immune to reasoned refutation. Their reality is unrecognizable as reality. And adding to our disorientation is that we see many people accommodate themselves to it.

The dark possibility spreading out from this epistemic gap is the end of politics. Given free rein, conspiracism augurs not an end to government—coercion by state officials will continue, after all—but an end to politics. Politics is the clash of competing interests and opinions, joined to argumentation and negotiation, from which collective decisions emerge. It is shaped by processes and institutions judged legitimate. But politics is also the arena in which the common sense of ordinary people sets the terms of a shared reality. We are far from the end of politics. But this is what is at stake in the assault on democratic foundations—on parties and knowledge—and in the war on common sense that gives life to the unsettling question, Who owns reality?

Fabulation

The challenge of alternate reality arose in a pointed way in the summer of 2018, when supporters began to appear at Trump rallies carrying signs and wearing shirts with the block letter *Q* printed on them. The signs referred to the QAnon conspiracy we mentioned in chapter 1, a conspiracy so convoluted as to almost defy description. Here is a summary. It begins with Pizzagate, the allegation that Hillary Clinton and her campaign chairman colluded in an international child sex ring centered in a Washington, DC, pizzeria. It then extends the Pizzagate plot by casting every president since Ronald Reagan as a participant in child sex trafficking. Every president, that is, except Trump—who alone is taking on a "worldwide ring of blackmailers" that includes these child sex traffickers, as well as liberal globalists and Jewish bankers. According to QAnon, the Mueller investigation into Russian interference in the 2016 election is itself a ruse. Actually, according to QAnon, Trump and the special prosecutor are acting together to distract attention from their secret plan to shut down the ring, which has infiltrated the US government. The day of reckoning is approaching when Trump will declare open war on the conspiracy, assisted by John F. Kennedy Jr., who faked his death and will now return. Tens of thousands of arrests will be made and thousands of corporate CEOs will resign. Their covert rule will be ended, their secret power overturned, and Hillary Clinton will be locked up. "This is what draining the swamp looks like," says one poster on the 8chan message board. QAnon is about a conspiracy to thwart a conspiracy.[10]

QAnon's development is instructive. It began with posts on the 4chan message board left by "Q," putatively an anonymous government employee who claimed high-level access to the secret plan. Message boards like 4chan and 8chan are virtual communities where conspiracists gather and exchange suspicions and conjectures. Q posts his clues, or "crumbs," as they are called, and anonymous posters step in to unpack their meaning. The rambling, expansive, incoherent character of the conspiracy reflects its origins in hundreds and thousands of separate "researchers" who analyze and "validate" Q's clues.[11] For instance, a photograph of Trump receiving a basketball jersey from the University of Alabama with the number seventeen on it is taken as verification of the Q conspiracy—the letter *Q* is the seventeenth in the alphabet. In fact, the number refers to the year 2017, and the same team gave President Barack Obama a jersey bearing the number fifteen in 2015.[12] The process mimics collaboration and peer review: someone posts a hypothesis and others ignore it, reject it, or accept it. Something is accepted when others on the board repeat it and build on it. This is the endpoint of the new conspiracist process at work: bare assertion validated by affirmation—by "a lot of people are saying"—culminating in a piling up of fabulation on fabulation.

Like much of the new conspiracism, QAnon began with conspiracy entrepreneurs. Investigators at NBC traced its source to two message board moderators at 4chan who reached out to Tracy Diaz, a conspiracy entrepreneur whose videos had a small YouTube following. Diaz posted videos about the conspiracy and her stock rose: as she said, "Because I cover Q, I got a fan base." Her videos, viewed over eight million times, became her source of income. Meanwhile, the 4chan moderators built a following as well. They moved discussions to Reddit, from which they then jumped to Facebook, which in turn steered a much larger audience to 4chan. And they started a 24/7 YouTube channel that offered viewers all QAnon, all the time, and that they used to collect donations.[13]

QAnon is so preposterous, it is tempting to ignore it. As critic Tim Smith-Laing put it, QAnon "is so Byzantine in the labyrinth it has constructed around itself it's laughable."[14] QAnon's following was not large. But as celebrities like Roseanne Barr and Curt Schilling endorsed QAnon, it grew. Its reach was amplified when followers who showed up at Trump rallies with signs and shirts saying "We Are Q," got national press coverage. QAnon shows the new conspiracism moving from once obscure message boards to the most visible public spaces of democratic life.

The details of QAnon illustrate how the new conspiracism has brought us into a fight over the basic elements of reality and prompt the disorienting recognition that common sense is no longer common. What we see at a Trump rally where people hold up Q signs is not only the fact that we inhabit different realities but also an indicator of the intention of some to make their distorted sense of reality a public affair. QAnon is not dispassionate; it is the fighting face of the most bizarre conspiracist narratives in politics. What if QAnon or a concoction like it spreads? What if the question QAnon followers ask at the Trump rallies—"Are you with us?"—takes hold in electoral politics? What if the demand is made of candidates and officials to affirm this compromised account of reality? What if challenges to common sense increase and increasingly shape political life?

We think that QAnon represents an ephemeral element at the fringe of popular political culture. Still, we see in it the new conspiracist claim to own reality, and we see how verification is a matter of repetition and assent. We see the assault on common sense. Our own sense, however, is that common sense can prove more formidable than the forceful ascent of the new conspiracism might have us believe.

Common Sense as Resistance

The very thing that is at stake here—common sense—is also a resource for protecting democracy against conspiracism. It always has been. The idea of common sense has a political history rooted in the philosophy of the Scottish Enlightenment, inserted into the Declaration of Independence in the form of "self-evident truths," and popularized in the most important American revolutionary tract, Thomas Paine's *Common Sense*.[15]

Paine's great pamphlet offers us a model of common sense as the basis of democracy and as the touchstone of resistance—in his case against the malignant normality of colonial rule.

Paine addressed his pamphlet to ordinary Americans throughout the colonies; an estimated 150,000 copies were circulated. His task was to persuade the people that the goal of the revolution should not be limited to repealing oppressive policies. Rather than reconciliation, the revolution should aim at independence and a democratic republic. "Common sense is firmly on the side of the people and thus opposed to the rulership of kings,"[16] Paine wrote, and he dissected all the inaccessible, mystifying elements of monarchic and colonial ideology. "Under how many subtleties, or absurdities, has the divine right to govern been imposed on the credulity of mankind," he wrote, and set out to dispel these subtleties and absurdities. He was the consummate rhetorician of common sense, turning royalist obfuscations upside down—"There is something very absurd, in supposing a continent to be perpetually governed by an island."[17] And against the traditionalist British claim that age confers wisdom, he commended youth as the seed time of good habits.

Paine fueled American political outrage by teaching that the British claims to rule were an assault on Americans' common sense, understood as the plain good sense of the many as opposed to the mystifications of an inherited nobility and the Crown. Common sense belongs to the people generally and contrasts with the obfuscation, hypocrisy, dogma, and demand for deference that come from authorities who use their claim to esoteric knowledge to prevent ordinary people from questioning their authority. It refers to shared experience as the basis for those things everyone can be expected to know. The first accent is on *common*, then, the sense of things shared by the great mass of people. Like philosophers of common sense before him, Paine insisted that a true grasp of things is accessible to everyone. All that Americans needed to understand the reality of their political situation—the malice directed at them and what must be done—was plain speech and deliberation among themselves about what was going on and what common sense directed them to do.

Paine's accent falls equally on the second element of common sense—on *sensibility*—which points to common sense as an emotional and motivational force. The feelings of outrage Americans felt against the British, who oppressed them and against whom they were already in bloody conflict, were not only justified but irreversible. Once lost, deference cannot be regained. Enemy "extinguishes every other name and title," Paine wrote.[18] Common sense made political independence emotionally inevitable. Early in American history, then, common sense was invoked during a crisis of political legitimacy, and its import was self-protective and democratic. And from then to now, assaults on common sense have aroused in many strong emotions and something like visceral resistance.

In the eighteenth century, Paine's *Common Sense* was a rallying cry and a resource in the fight against the willfulness and arbitrariness of a king who had his own view of political reality and who imposed it on the colonies. Today, common sense is a resource for fighting the new conspiracists, who also claim to own reality. When conspiracism takes hold in a president who has the scope of power captured by the phrase "the imperial presidency," we are right to see presidential conspiracism as willful, arbitrary rule.[19] We are right to invoke Paine and counterpose common sense to conspiracism. Paine's confidence in common sense made American independence possible. Common sense is necessary to protect democracy today.

Common sense operates at a deep level, undergirding our institutions and supporting our sense of being a people. Historian Gordon Wood argued that the success of the United States over time owes less to the great founding document of the Constitution or to the country's institutional arrangements, as so many have argued. Rather, it owes to "the common sense of the American people throughout our entire history, and our continued success will depend upon that common sense."[20] We hear a note of democratic optimism whenever common sense is invoked—just as we invoke it now as a bulwark against conspiracist claims to own reality. There are ways to resist conspiracism, and they strike us as matters of common sense. They are speaking truth to conspiracy and enacting democracy, and they are the subject of chapter 7.

DEFENDING DEMOCRACY

In a dark time the eye begins to see.

THEODORE ROETHKE, "IN A DARK TIME"

7

Speaking Truth

A chasm separates those who assent to the accusations of the new conspiracism and those who cannot comprehend conspiracism's popular reception, much less its sway in halls of power, and who fear its consequences. We fear conspiracist assaults on the integrity of parties and elections and on the authority of knowledge-producing institutions. We fear the conscription of thought, violations of common sense, and conspiracists' claim to own reality. At stake in speaking truth to conspiracy is the reassertion of common sense and the stanching of the delegitimation of democracy.

If the stakes are high, so are the obstacles to refutation and repair. The closed conspiracist mind-set is immunized against contradictory evidence and argument, and invulnerable to correction. Speaking truth to conspiracy is hobbled by the fact that so many officials accommodate conspiracy charges and remain silent.

The most obvious answer to conspiracism would seem to be transparency: combat charges of secrecy with openness, so citizens can see and hear leaders at work. Since John Wilkes first published the proceedings of the British Parliament (and was sent to the Tower of London for doing so), faith in transparency has never wavered. Transparency has become a mantra invoked by ethicists, public officials, the media, advocacy groups that monitor government, and citizens hoping to hold representatives accountable.[1] The demand for transparency is all the more powerful because the national security state classifies far too much material and creates a background of secrecy that only a few are permitted to penetrate.[2] Doubtless this contributes to conspiracist tendencies to see what is secret as nefarious. Nevertheless, transparency works to prevent political corruption and misconduct. It is a deterrent. And transparency plays an indisputable part in facilitating political accountability. Transparency is now formally required in a variety of ways and extends to legislation, executive orders, regulations, court decisions, the data used in making decisions, the records of argument and reasons, and the authors of policy and names of those in opposition.

Yet transparency does not work automatically; on its own, publicity will not cure corruption or enable political accountability, nor will it ensure that even the most absurd conspiracist claims will be refuted.[3] Transparency "places it in the public domain, but does not guarantee that anybody will find it, understand it or grasp its relevance."[4] Everything made public must be brought to the attention of some part of the public. Everything must be interpreted. Who selects and frames interpretations? For what purpose, and what audience? The products of transparency can be manipulated and marketed, and conspiracists can twist and exploit the very materials transparency makes accessible.

Conspiracism flourishes today in our comparatively open democracy in spite of the regulations that compel a great deal of transparency. Official sources of information that are meant to dispel conspiratorial beliefs end up enhancing them—this happens, for instance, when official sources contain redactions.[5] But for conspiracists, documents released by government agencies or congressional committees are just more evidence of fabrication, hoax, and covers for impending coups. Transparency, the upside-down conspiracist argument goes, is itself a deception. In fact, however, conspiracism is not really a complaint about incomplete openness. It is not a demand for more transparency. When conspiracists attack "pretended transparency," it does not mean that they want true transparency. Conspiracism is not fundamentally concerned with anticorruption or accountability, the two purposes transparency serves.

Speaking truth to conspiracy is not a matter of making things more transparent. It is disarming when it is, because it uses verifiable information to support an interpretation of the actions of political men and women that makes sense of things to citizens. In the political theorist Pierre Rosanvallon's terms, we need legibility, not just transparency.[6]

So, who speaks truth to conspiracy, or should? What is effective truth speaking, anyway? What entrenched obstacles inhibit speaking out and, often enough, then renders it toothless? What else do we need to disarm conspiracism and repair its effects?

The Texas Takeover Conspiracy

The first obstacle to contesting conspiracism is reticence—refusal to speak out. Consider, for instance, the so-called military takeover of Texas of 2015. Often, when conspiracy theorists charge the government with gross malfeasance—alleging, for instance, that the federal government plotted the bombing of the Pentagon and World Trade Center in 2001 or that John F. Kennedy's assassination was the product of CIA meddling in Cuba—knowledgeable government representatives have defended an official version of the event, buttressed by evidence, investigations, and reports. But in the summer of 2015, when some Texans came to believe that the United States Army was plotting to invade the state, officials instead signaled their sympathy for those who suspected a conspiracy. The Texas takeover conspiracy began when the United States Army announced that it would be staging a summer military training exercise stretching across seven western and southwestern states. Called Jade Helm 15, the exercise was intended to train special forces to operate in unfamiliar terrain. The army released an unintentionally provocative map that labeled Texas, Utah, and southernmost California "enemy" territory and Colorado, Nevada, and most of California "friendly" territory; the "enemy" was red and the "friendly" territory, blue.[7]

The unhappy coincidence, which the military should have foreseen, is that 2008 and 2012 election maps showed Republican states in red and Democratic states in blue. As a result, the announcement of the training exercise, along with the accompanying map, immediately excited conspiracist suspicions. Alex Jones expertly fertilized such fears with his insistence that the army planned to take over Texas, disarm the population, and jail key political leaders, who, in Texas, were Republicans. He later refined his charge to hold that the army was preparing the population for an eventual takeover by habituating people to the sight of soldiers and military equipment in civilian areas. By then the story had escalated: the United States Army was not merely going to invade and occupy Texas but was also going to disarm the population and impose martial law.[8]

In itself, that a secretive army training exercise taking place in civilian areas—a plan accompanied by maps that mirrored the partisan divide in the country—might arouse suspicion is not altogether surprising. What was extraordinary was the reaction of numerous public officials. Leaders like Greg Abbott, the governor of Texas, did not try to calm popular fears or resist conspiracist delusions with reasonable explanations based on their knowledge of events. Instead, officials signaled that they, too, had concerns. Abbott went so far as to task the Texas State Guard with monitoring the military operation on behalf of the state: "During the training operation," Abbott wrote to the guard, "it is important that Texans know their safety, constitutional rights, private property rights and civil liberties will not be infringed."[9] While Abbott's letter elicited ridicule elsewhere in the nation, he was not the only official to go along with conspiracist stories.[10] As Texas congressman Louie Gohmert said, "The map of this exercise needs to change, the names on the map need to change, and the tone of the exercise needs to be completely revamped so the federal government is not intentionally practicing war against its own states."[11] Abbott chose not to speak truth to conspiracy: as one Republican former Texas state representative wrote, Abbott should make decisions based on "facts and evidence" and stop "pandering to idiots."[12]

The governor's complicity in conspiracism was rooted in the partisan connection. To the extent that his own supporters and constituents believed that the army was planning to invade Texas, Abbott was under pressure to show that he not only understood their worries but also shared them. And that is where the failure lies. To understand a worry is in some sense to acknowledge that the worry is reasonable. It takes rhetorical care to both communicate that one understands what people think and also correct it. By representing himself as sharing the worry of a military takeover, he failed to fulfill his responsibility to not only express an understanding but also correct a *mis*understanding by telling his constituents that their fears are unfounded and dangerous. He abdicated his responsibility to maintain a partisan connection that works in two directions. The two-way connection transmits information not only from the citizens to government but also from the government to citizens.

Most people stand at a distance from the institutions of government, especially when government acts on a continental scale. Washington, DC, is a long way from Midland, Texas—geographically and culturally. The partisan connection is the principal tether linking ordinary citizens and the national government—including the leaders who plan military exercises like Jade Helm. It is the responsibility of representatives to call on that connection—to strengthen the tether by acknowledging popular fears, but at the same time, to speak the truth. Top to bottom, the governor, members of Congress, and state legislators failed in this obligation, and failed the people of Texas.

The Partisan Connection

Let's look closely at the partisan connection and its significance for conspiracism. As we discussed in chapter 4, parties link the social pluralism we find in a free society to the formal institutions of government. They organize the pluralist array of interests and opinions and bring them into public life. To serve that purpose, parties have to connect to popular views on the ground. In part, this is a matter of organization: elected officials and party leaders are organized territorially to connect to constituents and partisan supporters at every level, from national arenas to street-corner society. They must be responsive not only to an undefined public but also to particular groups and associations, their constituents, their supporters, and potential supporters. Representatives need to look and sound as if they might share popular sensibilities. The more suspicious their constituents are of government, the more representatives will need to address their mistrust. They need to educate citizens about government and offer true explanations of public actions while refuting unwarranted ones. When it is unwarranted to think that the military is planning to take over Texas, democratically elected representatives need to say so, plainly. Yet at the same time these same leaders need to acknowledge the fears of the people they represent. They need to connect.

This connection is sometimes sustained by recognizing that conspiracism comes with the imprimatur of the foundational democratic demand for "eternal vigilance." If government were in fact wholly trustworthy and every conspiracist claim were false, we could attribute all conspiracist thinking to paranoia or bad faith. But skepticism is always warranted, and some conspiracist claims are true. The trust that representatives cultivate enables them to assuage fears and convince citizens that a particular conspiracy claim is indeed false. Insofar as conspiracist stories are spread and adopted because of their source—because people identify with the person (now including the president) or social group pushing the narrative of secret agents and malignant intent—only another compelling source with which people identify can get attention. When representation works well, officials can fill that role.

When it works, the partisan connection, which is the soul of political representation, goes in two directions. In one direction, representatives transmit and crystallize the interests, views, desires, and fears of voters and bring them into the formal institutions of government. In the other direction, representatives educate voters' interests and address their fears.

The partisan connection is not working well today. The new conspiracism, as we've noted, has a partisan penumbra that aligns it with the extreme right. As we said in chapter 4, we see an alignment between conservative ideology, which draws its energy from antigovernmentalism and anti-internationalism, on the one hand, and the rash of conspiracist claims about the "deep state" and betrayal of real Americans, on the other. The partisan penumbra means that Republican officials have a presumptive advantage in comparison to Democrats or nonpartisan civil servants in refuting conspiracist claims. Their corrections are more likely to elicit trust from conservatives and Republicans in the electorate. But what we see today are elected Republican officials who, instead of speaking truth, calculate that their own electoral survival and the success of their favored policies are better ensured by acquiescing to conspiracism. There is a virtually united front of elected officials, donors, and partisan activists. And so, representatives placate, avoid questions, refrain from comment, utter platitudes, and remain silent. Some affirm conspiracist claims themselves.

Of course, obstacles to speaking out are strongest when conspiracist charges are leveled against the political opposition. Every Republican felt compelled to affirm, for instance, the allegation that Hillary Clinton conspired as secretary of state to cover up the details of the 2012 attack on the American mission in Benghazi, Libya, in which ambassador J. Christopher Stevens was killed. The partisan imperative to attack Clinton overwhelmed the need to both get at the facts and speak truth about them. This is undiluted partisan reticence.

Representatives accommodated themselves to conspiracism's malignant normality.

Failure to speak truth to conspiracy changes the complexion of the partisan connection. Rooted in calculations of electoral survival and party loyalty, reticence raises the question in constituents' minds, indeed in the public mind, whether party leaders and representatives mean what they say. When are they accommodating conspiracism in bad faith? When are they actively peddling stories they know are false? When are they pandering to and exploiting popular fears or donors' threats? Can they be trusted when it comes to fundamental untruths that degrade democracy?

Conspiracism brings us face to face with both the partisan connection and the limits of the hold that partisanship should have on democratically elected representatives. The character of representatives is revealed by how they respond to threats, and conspiracy claims present palpable tests of their moral mettle. They must be willing to point out that conspiracist claims are false even when these claims also function as an attack on the opposition party, just as they must hold their own party accountable for condescending to conspiracism. They must be willing to step out of the partisan penumbra, to loosen or cut the partisan connection, to say, as Senator Jeff Flake did, "We are not here simply to mark time. Sustained incumbency is certainly not the point of seeking office and there are times when we must risk our careers in favor of our principles. Now is such a time."[13]

Political Representatives: The First Line of Defense

Speaking truth to conspiracy is a moral and political imperative, and it is a sign of dangerous times that so few responsible officeholders do. Consider Representative John Ratcliffe's charge in January 2018: "We learned today about information that in the immediate aftermath of his election, there may have been a 'secret society' of folks within the Department of Justice and the FBI . . . working against [Donald Trump]." Ratcliffe continued, "I'm not saying that actually happened."[14] Two days later, after the ominous text message about a "secret society" was widely identified as a joke between two FBI employees rather than evidence of a plot, another Republican, Senator Ron Johnson, backed off and allowed that it might have been written in jest. But still he equivocated: "It's a real possibility," Johnson said.[15] This falls short of disavowal of a conspiracy within the FBI, clearly, and falls shorter still of a sober defense of the agency or the Justice Department. And the conspiracist purpose has been achieved. Doubts are planted, and a share of the country will discount anything federal law enforcement says about FBI investigations, particularly as regards Trump. Such officeholders are contributing to the delegitimation of a crucial government institution and the rule of law.

Some do have the integrity to speak truth. At a 2008 rally when John McCain was running against Barack Obama for the presidency, a questioner confessed to McCain that she felt she could not trust Obama because "he's an Arab." At the time, the birther conspiracy was dogging the Obama campaign. McCain, however—eliciting boos from his own supporters—refused to indulge the forces of delegitimation. "No, ma'am: no, ma'am," McCain said. "He's a decent family man, a citizen that I just happen to have disagreements with on fundamental issues, and that's what this campaign is all about. He's not."[16]

Another example of speaking truth comes in the speech we mentioned earlier by Flake, when he condemned both Trump's behavior and partisan reticence. "It is time for our complicity and our accommodation of the unacceptable to end," Flake insisted. Invoking the first-person plural, "we," he refers both to his fellow legislators in general and to his party: "Were the shoe on the other foot, we Republicans—would we Republicans meekly accept such behavior on display from dominant Democrats? Of course, we wouldn't, and we would be wrong if we did." He went on, "When we remain silent and fail to act . . . because we might make enemies, because we might alienate the base, because we might provoke a primary challenge, because ad infinitum, ad nauseam . . . we dishonor our principles and forsake our obligations."[17]

McCain's action and Flake's speech were widely noted and admired, but neither received public affirmation from other Republicans in Congress. Flake's Senate speech was not followed by a raft of promises (not even just a few) vowing, "I will not be complicit or silent."

Can we expect this kind of principled opposition to conspiracism and allied pathologies of lying and vilification to get attention outside Washington, DC, and beyond its moment? Looking back, we may find that there was a right time, a moment of "opening," when personal witnessing and a phalanx of speaking out really stanched conspiracism or its effects. Perhaps speeches like these, even if they didn't motivate others to follow in the moment, nonetheless opened some minds.

Speaking truth to conspiracy is not just for political representatives, of course. We rely on the press as well. Our capacity as citizens, and indeed the capacity of officials, to dispute conspiracist claims depends on arduous reporting and credible sources. Experts, too, both inside and outside government, whose authority derives from special knowledge, must speak out—as scientists do in the case of climate change when they educate, advocate, and mobilize, taking on the role of "witnessing professionals."[18] Civil society groups speak truth to conspiracy as a regular part of their work. Some defend the rights of groups that conspiracists scapegoat, such as migrants. Private citizens speak out personally and individually, too, in a host of informal settings where "a lot of people are saying" is critically assessed.

Still, as a practical matter, political officials are the sine qua non when it comes to answering conspiracism. Courts protect against many violations of constitutional law and, of course, uphold due process in criminal proceedings. They are bulwarks against some of the cruelest and most arbitrary measures against migrants—separation of children from their parents, for example, by executive order. And these measures themselves come wrapped up in conspiracist claims. But judges do not "speak truth to conspiracy." When political representatives have it both ways by passively acquiescing in conspiracist charges and avoiding straightforward refutation, no other institution can step in and do what they will not. When only a handful of Republicans break ranks with conspiracists in their party and with the conspiracist president, when they exhibit so-called loyalty and present "the image of a unified party," when they fail to disrupt the exacerbated polarized political dynamics that are now epistemic as well as partisan, they implicitly accept these claims.[19] They do not even try to build coalitions across the political spectrum to oppose conspiracism. They fail to do what they might in spite of the fact that conspiracism is infecting and distorting the business of their own institution, the United States Congress.

Speaking truth to conspiracy underscores the discipline required of partisanship and political representation. We speak of discipline advisedly because, like all discipline, it is a felt experience, arduous and uncomfortable. Discipline requires officials to recognize threats to democratic legitimacy in absurd stories concocted from whole cloth. It requires the effort to recognize in the surface noise of democratic politics what is genuinely damaging.[20] Speaking truth to conspiracism as both a moral matter and a political responsibility requires officials to risk retribution from their own party leadership. Some conspiracist charges require them to step outside the partisan penumbra even if it means loosening the partisan connection, and even if it means electoral defeat.

Getting through to Open Minds

Representatives must overcome reticence, refuse to acquiesce, and speak truth to conspiracy, but still there are impediments to stanching the dangerous claims that delegitimate democracy. With all conspiracism, classic and new, the counterstrategy of speaking truth runs up against the wall of closed minds. With classic conspiracism—the kind that collects evidence, that tries to connect all the dots, that offers theories and explanations—speaking truth to conspiracy is often ineffective. The conspiracist's sealed mind-set is resistant to intervention. Conspiracists categorize contrary evidence as part of the conspiracy itself, and competing evidence is especially suspect when it comes from the very sources said to be part of the plan: political officials or government commissions or the mainstream press.

These qualities of mind—epistemic closure, or a self-sealing resistance to all challenging facts—also make the new conspiracism difficult to correct and contest. It is all the more difficult in the case of the new conspiracism because so often the "evidence" consists only of bare assertion, "a lot of people are saying." In addition, there's the tribal element of the new conspiracism: identification with a group for which conspiracist stories are a regular way of viewing the political world. The tribal element imposes a real cost on changing one's mind. Call it the reputational obstacle to acknowledging false belief.

This consideration lies behind a proposal by law professors Cass Sunstein and Adrian Vermeule for reaching "hard-core" holders of false beliefs: they suggest infiltrating conspiracist groups. "Planting doubts" and "introducing beneficial cognitive diversity" is their prescription for repairing conspiracists' "crippled epistemology." Government, on this view, should attempt to "debias or disable its purveyors" in this fashion.[21] Their proposal for a government-sponsored conspiracy to combat conspiracy recalls the efforts by J. Edgar Hoover, the founding director of the FBI, who ran a counterintelligence program from 1956 to 1971 that, among other illegal and improper techniques, infiltrated civil rights groups.[22] Infiltrating conspiracist groups is a similar offense against civil liberties—especially when the group is not a terrorist cell or some other violent association. Today, like-minded people who create and spread conspiracist ideas form networks transformed by the revolution in communications technology. They are not groups in the sense of face-to-face associations, in contrast to the Montana militia, for instance, but are networks digitally dispersed across the world. Anyone is free to participate in the online discussions. But were the government to infiltrate such discussions (and we now see that this has indeed been done, including by a hostile foreign government, using a variety of camouflages), the effort would sooner or later be exposed. The result would be to fertilize and presumptively justify the very conspiracism it intends to combat.

The law professors propose to fight fire with fire: to conspire against conspiracy. But sometimes the best way to fight this fire is with water: to meet conspiracist charges with whatever truth we can command, pronounced openly and plainly. Correction emerges from a process of submitting propositions to the scrutiny of evidence dispassionately and meticulously collected. Yet this process—mimicked by classic conspiracism and repudiated by the new conspiracism—is unlikely to be effective for those who assent to fabulations. With respect to them, one can hardly exaggerate the depth of the authority deficit that afflicts anyone claiming to be in a position of knowledge. The delegitimation of knowledge-producing institutions has been effective. As one penitent conservative lamented, "The gatekeepers have lost all credibility in the minds of consumers, I don't see how you reverse it."[23]

The problem is not only that gatekeepers have lost authority but also that the gatekeeping function itself has almost disappeared. As priestly epistemic authority over the word of God was displaced by the fifteenth-century invention of the movable-type printing press and the subsequent printing of the Bible in vernacular languages, so contemporary authorities have been sidelined by digital technology, which allows anyone to disseminate words and images at very little cost. When publication was very expensive, scholars, editors, and publishers exercised an unavoidable gatekeeping function: they decided what was worthy of dissemination. When the limited spectrum of public airways was the only way to broadcast voice and video, producers could decide what was worthy of being aired. Now there is no limit to the text and images that can be broadcast over Twitter, Facebook, YouTube, and websites like Infowars. As the volume of what can be communicated approaches infinity and the cost approaches zero, the conventional gatekeeping function recedes.

Apple, Google, Facebook, and other platforms have tiptoed into gatekeeping. In the summer of 2018 they removed conspiracist content produced by Alex Jones and his site Infowars. In justifying its decision, Facebook said that Jones violated its community standards by "glorifying violence" and "using dehumanizing language to describe people who are transgender, Muslim, and immigrants."[24] Facebook would not reveal how it categorized the violation, nor how many times Jones's Facebook pages ran afoul of the community standards before the content was removed. In contrast to the traditional media like newspapers, Facebook's editorial function is both opaque and diffident. It is as if the company wants to pretend that it can remain just a tool people use to connect, rather than acknowledging its status as the twenty-first-century equivalent of the newspaper and the network news broadcast. As a result of identifying itself only as a profit-maximizing corporation, rather than also as a public trust, the company has been slow to recognize its civic responsibility and the difficult decisions that entails.

Still, it is possible that Facebook and companies like it will recreate some kind of gatekeeping function. Already, they are fitfully moving away from a passive posture of openness that permits anyone to post anything. Even now, Facebook employs "third-party fact checkers" who assess the accuracy of articles in the News Feed.[25] It is possible that fact checking will develop into a profession with its own internal standards, its own ethics, and its own professional modes of certification and testing. If the profession develops and is integrated into digital platforms like Facebook, the gatekeeping function could be refashioned.

We may well be skeptical that any new epistemic authority could succeed when it comes to closed conspiracist minds. But meeting the political challenge does not require persuading everyone; it only requires reaching open minds. And the challenge here is not only the decline of gatekeeping but also the corollary problem of information overload. Given the staggering frequency and velocity of conspiracist charges, the burden of speaking truth is incessant, which itself may become fatiguing. It can wear out both those who are challenging conspiracism and ordinary citizens who have to keep up.

The difficulty of capturing attention also owes to asymmetry: conspiracy without the theory deals in sound bites: "Rigged!" It is easy to state, spread, and swallow. It flows here and there through the capillaries of public culture. Refutation of faulty facts and examination of faulty claims are not "sexy": "The debunk seldom travels as far as the conspiracy claim and, indeed, it can help keep the claim conspicuous."[26]

Scholars of misinformation have argued that refutation and denial may sometimes have the unintended effect of reinforcing the very conspiracist belief that is being discredited. As we noted in chapter 2, in the most vexing cases, actively rebutting conspiracist charges may have the effect of cementing them in people's minds—this is called the "backfire effect."[27] On this view, erroneous understanding is amplified in the process of refutation. So it is not surprising to find some political observers arguing that the best strategy is to ignore conspiracism and its cousin falsehoods and lies, on grounds that, in practice, the act of rebuttal underscores conspiracist claims and gives them a degree of credibility.[28] Yet recent studies show that corrections can be absorbed, or at least they may not have the perverse backfire effect of strengthening the views they are meant to refute.[29] Fact checking can increase the reputational costs for political officials who disregard the accuracy of their state-ments.[30] A reasonable conclusion is that to diagnose the threat that conspiracism poses, to unravel its logic, to falsify its spe-cific claims, to call out the conspiracists, and to point to its de-structive consequences are all necessary, though they are not guaranteed to disarm it.

But the strategy of speaking truth, even when it makes a dif-ference, is insufficient if it is not accompanied by political action. The idea that all one needs to do is describe things as accurately as possible points to an unexpected symmetry be-tween the new conspiracism and the strategy of speaking truth: both hold that declarations are enough to save the nation or change the world. For new conspiracists, it's as if invoking a malignant plot is enough. All the energy is in declaring, repeat-ing, and affirming ruses. Exposing per se is all the work that needs to be done. The point of symmetry lies here, in the thought that exposing the faults in conspiracist claims is all that need be done. There is little reason to put all our faith in the efficacy of exposure, if unmasking and revealing don't prompt additional action. "What is the basis for assuming that it [exposure] will surprise or disturb, never mind motivate, anyone to learn that a given social manifestation is artificial, self-contradictory . . . phantasmatic, or even violent?"[31] When conspiracism begins to appear normal, and when it hijacks institutions and inverts democratic processes, relegitimating democracy requires more than speaking truth. It demands a reassertion of standard demo-cratic ways of going about the business of politics.

Enacting Democracy

Speaking truth to conspiracism is an effort to contain its ef-fects. But refutation is one thing; relegitimation is another. Reversing the damage done to the meaning, value, and authority of democratic institutions is its own challenge. What we call enacting democracy is a way to not merely contain the force of conspiracism but also to relegitimate democratic institutions. Performed over and over, it has a cumulative effect. It is not what busy officials normally do. In fact, it is difficult to find examples of it because it simply has not been seen as necessary. But enacting democracy is what they can and should do now.

By *democratic enactment*, we mean more than faithful adherence to the regular political and legal processes of constitutional democracy. In addition, it entails a literal articulation of how each step in the process of legislating, prosecuting, regulating, or investigating (or even campaigning) adheres to fair processes. Enacting democracy entails attesting to the value of these practices. It explains what regular processes are about and, in the course of explaining, demonstrates and avows commitment to them. We're talking about politics as pedagogy.

Enacting democracy is more than giving justifications for decisions. To be sure, justification is the focus of a great deal of academic democratic theory, especially theories of deliberation. These focus on offering reasons that all can accept as the standard for decision-making—as if all of democracy were an extended legislative debate about particular policies. But democracy is also about institutions, not just deliberation. It involves delineated lines of authority and regular processes. We've shown that conspiracism distorts institutional practices. Under these conditions, enacting democracy—upholding regular processes and explaining them—is essential.

Relegitimation is a slow, extended affair. For it to take hold, citizens need to witness exhibitions of institutional integrity. An exemplary instance of enacting democracy occurred after Trump created the spurious Presidential Advisory Commission on Election Integrity. The commission was tasked, in effect, with confirming his conspiracist claim that massive voter fraud, on the order of three million illegal ballots, accounts for his loss of the popular vote. Trump's signature claim has no basis in fact and has been conclusively rebutted. With minor exceptions and the expected errors in record keeping (failing to differentiate people with the same name, failing to remove deceased individuals from the rolls, failing to record moves out of state, and so on), voter fraud allegations investigated by states, by social scientists, and by journalists have been discounted. As one team of political scientists put it, "The best estimate of the percentage of noncitizens who vote is zero."[32] Another group of researchers reports that "the expansive voter fraud concerns espoused by Donald Trump and those allied with him are not grounded in any observable features of the 2016 election."[33]

Kris Kobach, the Republican Kansas secretary of state who is identified as "the man behind Trump's voter-fraud obsession," and who is a fierce champion of punitive voting restrictions, was appointed vice-chair of the commission.[34] His history of inventing legal obstacles to registration and voting, of disenfranchising voters over technicalities, and of intimidating would-be voters should have been disqualifying.[35] But we are no longer surprised by the hijacking of institutions for conspiracist purposes or the manufacture of ad hoc arenas for "investigating" conspiracist allegations. The commission is a prime example of a "quixotic search for nonexistent evidence."[36]

What followed was an encouraging enactment of democracy as resistance to conspiracism. The commission demanded that every state turn over its complete voter files (including every voter's name, address, date of birth, voter history from

2006 on, party identification, voting records, military status, overseas citizen information, prosecution for electoral crimes, and felony convictions, as well as the last four digits of each voter's Social Security number). It also announced an intention to make this information public. Almost every state refused to hand over its data. Some states sent only publicly available information; others would not comply at all. New York governor Andrew Cuomo, a Democrat, said his state "refuses to perpetuate the myth [that] voter fraud played a role in our election."[37] The commission has also been sued by a privacy watchdog group and civil rights and voting rights groups. Those who resisted the commission and explained why—governors, secretaries of state, and citizen groups—enacted democracy. It was effective: in January 2018, the president precipitously disbanded the commission.

Enacting democracy is vital even when it is not aimed at combatting specific conspiracist charges. Consider the US attorney who, in the face of political pressure to subvert regular practice, explained the legal process of criminal prosecution. On Halloween night in 2017, Sayfullo Saipov, a legal US resident, used a rented truck to strike cyclists, pedestrians, and a school bus in a terrorist attack in New York City. Eight people died and others were wounded. Trump went immediately on Twitter to say, "Send him to Gitmo!"—the controversial detention facility at Guantanamo, Cuba, that falls outside the regular justice system. The president called our system of justice a "joke" and a "laughingstock." He demanded capital punishment for "the animal."[38]

The day after the attack, Joon H. Kim, the acting US attorney for the Southern District of New York, made a public appearance to explain to a stunned national audience the charges quickly brought against Saipov. He commended the FBI and other law enforcement agencies for their swift action. Agents had collected the perpetrator's cell phones—"conducted pursuant to a court ordered wiretap," Kim carefully added. Agents had interrogated the suspect and gotten a confession in what was, Kim carefully added, a "Mirandized interview." He reminded viewers of the number of infamous terrorists who had been successfully prosecuted and sentenced through the regular federal system. He did not mention Trump or his delegitimating attacks on the system of justice.[39] He did not have to. He enacted the role of responsible US attorney. He exhibited dignity and confidence in legal due processes.[40] It was a moment of democratic pedagogy.

Enacting democracy can require officials to confront delegitimating conspiracism personally as well as officially when they become its targets. Embattled FBI deputy assistant director Peter Strzok became a target of attack when private emails he exchanged with his girlfriend during the 2016 election became public and showed him casting aspersions on Trump (as well as other candidates). Strzok was drawn into the broader attack on the Justice Department and FBI leveled by the president and his congressional allies who saw the investigation of Russian intervention in US elections as part of a conspiracy within the government. They cast Strzok as part of that organized conspiracy. Called to testify before a hostile Republican-led House Judiciary and Oversight Committee, Strzok went beyond a defensive disavowal of personal wrongdoing. He detailed the institutional safeguards—the entrenched procedures and hierarchy of accountability—that guard against politicization in the Justice Department: "At every step, at every investigative decision, there were multiple layers of people above me, assistant director, deputy director, director of the F.B.I., and multiple layers of people below me, section chiefs, unit chiefs and analysts, all of whom were involved in these decisions. They would not tolerate any improper behavior in me any more than I would tolerate it in them." Strzok explained that the normal practices of the department would prevent any individual from indulging his or her personal political preferences. "The suggestion that I, in some dark chamber in the F.B.I., would somehow cast aside all these procedures, all of these safeguards and do this is astounding to me. It couldn't happen."[41]

Strzok had become the canary in the coal mine: a measure of how the delegitimating force of conspiracism touches not only the Russia investigation but the entire Department of Justice. Of course, his description of close oversight within the department only confirmed conspiracists' notion that the plot really did involve the agency as a whole, the "deep state." Strzok, like other principals caught up in the conspiracy narrative, was aware of this: "I understand that my sworn testimony will not be enough for some people. . . . Many Americans are now skeptical of anything they hear out of Washington."[42] He did not expect his testimony to permeate conspiracists' closed minds. He intended to educate open minds. Strzok laid out what citizens may not have known but need to know about how internal hierarchical organization and entrenched processes are designed to ensure that due process is followed and the rule of law upheld. This is a fraught example because, in part, Strzok was defending himself. But in the context of malignant normality, it is a compelling instance of how officials can enact democracy.

Enacting democracy helps make government legible. As we said, fighting conspiracism is going to take more than transparency. Transparency has to do with publicizing the workings of officials, the day-to-day business of governing. Legibility is about making sense of power—identifying the holders of influence and the sources of their influence, understanding the material and cultural stakes of each political contest, and reading clearly who are the winners and losers of electoral and policy outcomes.[43] Enacting democracy helps citizens see all this. Political representatives and administrative officials committed to the pedagogy we call enacting democracy can do a lot to put power dynamics into sharp focus.

The business of classic conspiracism, warranted or not, was precisely to prove that the real configuration of power was concealed. The new conspiracism, with its innuendo and bare assertion, does not even try to make sense of power. And by delegitimating democratic institutions, the new conspiricism actually obscures power. When they work well, democratic institutions allow power relations to be correctly perceived. Officials who enact democracy take on the responsibility of ensuring that the clash of interests is visible; that the predictable impact of political decisions—the costs and benefits to different groups—is brought out for all to see. Enacting democracy makes politics legible. It is a force against conspiracism and its delegitimating effects.

The two activities to repair the damage of delegitimation—speaking truth to conspiracy and enacting democracy—do not call for heroic virtues. Senator Flake's speech about principled resistance was laudable, a fulfillment of an obligation he took on as a political representative, but it was not heroic. Losing an election or giving up a Senate seat is not a grave sacrifice. Nobody is being imprisoned, exiled, or killed. Electoral defeats and the electoral success of opposition candidates are modest, regular occurrences in democracy, and they should be seen that way. They define democracy. In the same way, US attorney Kim's public statement was an ordinary, low-key, public explanation of law enforcement practice that was notable only because of the extraordinary situation. We are fortunate; so far we don't need Albert Camus's rebel or courageous resistance fighters battling tyranny. We just need honest witnesses who speak truth to conspiracism and pay attention to the pedagogical moments built into everyday political life. So far, however, we have too few.

Conclusion

THE CRISIS OF DEMOCRACY

Democracy in the United States and Europe is threatened in ways few imagined possible only a short time ago. Many of us assumed that the democratic foundations laid after World War II and consolidated with the fall of the Berlin Wall in 1989 were unshakeable. Now they look less resilient. To some eyes, they appear fragile. As defenders of constitutional democracy, we find ourselves on the defensive. We thought that democracy had severe flaws, we recognized democratic deficits, but we believed in the possibility of reform. Was our confidence in the progressive arc of democracy premature, or naïve, or a sign that we were complacent because *we* were being well served, or perhaps utterly unfounded from the start? Did we underestimate antidemocratic forces brewing in society? The signs were there. For many years, public opinion polls had documented diminishing support for democratic institutions.[1] In the past two years, measures of civil and political freedom, which once had declined only in autocracies and dictatorships, took a turn for the worse: in 2016, "it was established that democracies . . . dominated the list of countries suffering setbacks."[2] Roberto Stefan Foa and Yascha Mounk give a name to this process: "deconsolidation."[3]

We have been startled into thought. The causes of political change can only be understood with hindsight, and we have little dispassionate distance. For us, right now, and not only in the United States, understanding begins with noting that "there's something happening here" and trying to grasp what that is. Galvanized by events, lawyers document disregard for the rule of law and constitutional limits; seasoned political observers record violations of informal democratic norms such as tolerance and restraint; journalists chronicle and correct the avalanche of official lies and falsehoods at the same time that they contend with threats to the independence of the press; psychiatrists point to dangerous patterns of overt derision and hostility toward individuals and whole groups by the president and other public officials; and civil rights organizations document an increase in hate crimes.

Scholars, too, spring into reflection. Some look for lessons from the past. Drawing on the history of democratic failings from Weimar Germany to Juan Perón's Argentina, political scientists identify the "guardrails" that keep democracy on track and the warning signs of incipient authoritarianism.[4] Political theorists return with new urgency to old questions about challenges to the moral foundations of constitutional democracy.[5]

The new conspiracism is but one entrant in the lineup of disruptive forces. In the United States, it has moved from the fringe and has taken up residence in the highest levels of government, and it makes an appearance in day-to-day political life. Our focus has not been the entire domain of conspiracism but rather those claims that strike at the heart of regular democratic politics: rigged elections, plans to impose martial law, depictions of political opponents as criminal, a Department of Justice planning a coup against the president.

David Runciman suggests that "the spread of conspiracy theories is a symptom of our growing uncertainty about where the threat really lies."[6] We have argued that the new conspiracism is itself a threat to democracy. In the context of what is referred to as the literature on "how democracies die," we don't propose the new conspiracism as a sufficient way of framing what is happening. The new conspiracism is not the engine of every crisis of democracy, nor does it figure in every crisis of democracy. Malignancy abounds, and not all degradations of democracy go together. The new conspiracism is more than simply an offshoot or epiphenomenon of other forces such as authoritarianism or strident populism. Once it secures a foothold in public life, conspiracism has independent force.

While classic conspiracy theories arise all over the world, as of now the new conspiracism is most evident in the United States. Even where classic conspiracy theories abound, there is little evidence of the kind of bare assertion and fabulist concoction that characterize the new conspiracism. But there is reason to think this will change. The developments we describe in the United States over the last decade are likely to come to the democracies of Europe, to India, and elsewhere. New communications technologies that eliminate the traditional gatekeeping functions of the media create an opening. Conspiracy entrepreneurs seize on this opening. So do opportunistic politicians. And the power that the new conspiracism can exert in politics is amplified, as we see, when political parties and other institutions are weakened and in disarray. Because all these factors are in play, the new conspiracism is unlikely to be contained to the United States.

Wherever it arises, the corrosive effects of the new conspiracism are distinctive: to delegitimate foundational democratic institutions and, in a more personal mode, to disorient us. Although disorientation is so widespread that it amounts to a collective condition, it is also ours personally and individually.

Disorientation

An obscure pizzeria in northwest Washington, DC, becomes, in the eyes of some, a center of international child sex trafficking run by Hillary Clinton's campaign chairman. A summer military training exercise becomes, in the eyes of some, an attempt by the United States Army to impose martial law on the state of Texas. The murder of twenty elementary school students in Newtown, Connecticut, becomes, in the eyes of some, a US government action designed to advance gun control legislation. An election without any notable irregularities adverse to the successful Republican nominee becomes, in the eyes of some (in particular, the president himself), a "rigged" election.

The frequency of such charges, the baffling quality of the narrative concoctions, and their free-floating nature, untethered as they are to anything observable in the real world, contribute to the new conspiracism's disorienting effect. We are disoriented by the realization that what is absurd to some is true enough to others. And we are talking not about evaluations of particular policies, in the way that a new tariff policy might seem sensible to some and nonsensical to others, but rather about basic perceptions of political reality. We have become accustomed to partisan polarization, the gap in the way

Democrats and Republicans evaluate public officials, public policies, and one another. The new conspiracism moves us from gap to chasm, for epistemic polarization ultimately dissolves our common sense of the world, as we discussed in chapter 6.

A shared world of basic perceptions and a shared sense of elemental causation—of what counts as plausible or farfetched—allows us to make ourselves understandable to each other even when we disagree. Disagreement may be many things: passionate, troubling, unpleasant, destructive, or even illuminating and productive. But in itself, it is not disorienting. On the contrary, to have a clear sense of what you disagree with is to have a political orientation. Knowing what we are against is often a more stable point of orientation than knowing what we are for. But under conditions in which we cannot make ourselves understandable to each other, disagreement itself becomes impossible. There will still be government, and it may preserve democratic forms, but it will be a political world in which we cannot understand each other.

Disorientation is a personal as well as collective condition. When those in power claim to own reality and impose their reality on public life, what happens to ours? What becomes of us as inhabitants of a common world that no longer seems a world in common? We experience anxiety, rage, and a sense of helpless confusion. Diagnosing disorientation is the first step in overcoming it.

Delegitimation

"I'm the only one that matters," the president says, in the course of dismissing an accumulation of high-level vacancies at the Department of State, crippling the backbone of US diplomacy.[7]

He is pointing not only to his extraordinary interpretation of executive authority but also, and just as ominously, to the belief that he needs to know nothing more than the content of his own mind. He calls the free press the "enemy of the people" and provokes violent confrontations with reporters. We have no need of those who do the hard work to excavate facts—it's all "fake news" anyway. He teaches his supporters to disdain experts—they all lend themselves to the service of global elites and to the deep-state conspiracy machinating against him. As for his opponents in elections? They too are enemies of the people. His opponent in the last election, the one he defeated in the Electoral College, should be "locked up."

This is the delegitimation of knowledge and the delegitimation of parties—and Donald Trump is only its most powerful agent. At every turn, the new conspiracism assaults the integrity and independence of knowledge-producing institutions. Perhaps because experts deal in specialized terms that often defy general understanding, they are politically vulnerable: they can be cast as a cabal. This is exactly what the new conspiracism does. Insofar as it delegitimates knowledge-producing institutions, conspiracism also incapacitates democratic government. And it does not proceed surgically; delegitimation extends across the board.

The delegitimation of parties also incapacitates democracy. As we see it today, the process starts by attacking particular candidates and party leaders as criminal or treasonous, extends to partisan opposition in general, and ultimately assaults parties and partisanship wholesale. This takes us back to a time before the idea of the legitimate opposition took hold. It reverts to a time before the acceptance that open, organized political opposition is essential to politics in pluralist societies and to political accountability. And it does not accept the regulated party rivalry that ensures a peaceful transfer of office. It takes us back to a time when parties were seen as conspiracies. For the new conspiracists, that is just what parties are, and they set out not only to make partisans impotent but in fact to delegitimate them.

Witnesses to the crisis of democracy often attempt to predict how democracies die or, in other terms, how they end. We do not think delegitimation is dramatic, like a political revolution, or sudden, like an executive order that in a stroke initiates a catastrophic or regime-changing policy. Conspiracist delegitimation is a way of hollowing out democracy. And it gives citizens new reasons to think that constitutional democracy cannot be made to work and is not theirs.

This is happening now. The delegitimation of parties prevents people from coming together after elections. The rituals of unity—concession speeches, inauguration ceremonies, State of the Union addresses—no longer function. They no longer give the losing side confidence that regular succession will hold and that the next election could carry their candidate to office—not if each side thinks the other is an illegitimate participant in public life. The delegitimation of knowledge-producing institutions deprives decision makers of elemental information they need to govern well. As the quality of public decisions degrades, citizens justifiably lose confidence that democratic government can serve the public interest, or even just their own interest.

Worst-Case Scenarios

What happens if the new conspiracism is sustained over many election cycles, over decades? What if the architecture of democracy is still standing but the meaning, value, and concern for the public good that lived within this framework have left the building?

Let's take a cold-eyed look at conceivable worst-case scenarios, beginning with disorientation.

What if Trump's admonition—"Just remember: what you're seeing and what you're reading is not what's happening"—is repeated over and over, over time?[8] A state of surprise and disorientation may not be personally sustainable. Some people will endure it and muster the resources to assert the shared grounds of common sense in their own lives and in public life. But others will avoid sustained disorientation by acquiescing in conspiracist narratives. They will adjust. They will accommodate. They will join the company of those for whom conspiracist charges are "true enough." The most likely scenario for most, however, will be tuning out: retreating into private life and distancing themselves emotionally from every bit of news about public life.[9] Call it resignation, or numbing.

Consider next a worst-case scenario for degraded knowledge-producing institutions. A recent study by the American Academy of Arts and Sciences reports that, when asked what comes to mind when they hear the phrase "scientific research," 52 percent of study participants were unable to give any response at all.[10] Project that into the future, recognizing that the peril is not just ignorance—itself a fatal incapacity when science is crucial for meeting catastrophic situations like climate change—but rejection of support for science altogether.

Malignant normality, we've argued, corrupts democracy by implicating officials who are just doing their jobs in the contorted reality of the new conspiracism. Malignant normality affects experts within government: their work is interfered with, their data are destroyed, and they are prevented from gathering new data. Their reports are ignored or rejected as hoaxes. Those who stand up for the integrity of their profession are hounded, sidelined, pushed out. The results can be disastrous—pandemics, for example, or government budgets untethered to calculations so that they result in recessions, or policies so ineptly designed and insufficient to meet problems that the result is the further collapse of systems of health care.

The worst-case scenario for political parties and elections is equally grim. Today the president of the United States asserts that his political opponents—the Democratic Party and its 2016 presidential nominee, Hillary Clinton—conspired to facilitate fraudulent voting and thus "rig" the presidential election. Fast-forward to a future election when Trump's political descendant is running for the presidency. And imagine that this candidate, on election night, is declared the loser. Imagine that in the hours after the election result is announced, the candidate does what Trump threatened to do if the election did not go his way—he or she refuses to concede. "I cannot concede because this election, like the last one, was rigged. In fact, I did not lose . . . and I will never concede."

In this scenario, the partisan reticence we described kicks in. Members of Congress issue noncommittal statements insisting, "Irregularities need to be investigated." The chief justice of the Supreme Court announces that he will not participate in the inauguration before getting to the bottom of these allegations even if the charges of a rigged election are free-floating, unspecific, and virtually impossible to investigate. But no matter; polls show that between 46 and 49 percent of the country—a number roughly equaling the percentage who voted for the losing candidate—believe the election was rigged.

Worst-case scenarios prompt some observers to caution, "Prepare for regime change, not policy change."[11] Other forces may result in replacing democracy with a rival regime, but for its part, the new conspiracism is not driving us toward authoritarianism or illiberal populism or neo-fascism. It is hollowing out democracy, not constructing something else. It is delegitimating democratic institutions. It is disorienting citizens. The question it raises is, Will citizens continue to recognize their own government as democratic? And then there is the question, Will they care?

What Next?

Two responses mitigate and contain the corrosive consequences of the new conspiracism. First is enacting democracy: a strenuous adherence to the regular processes and forms of public decision-making. Democracy is "enacted" when officials explicitly draw attention to the importance of adhering to these forms and practices. The way to demystify governmental power is to make the processes of legislation and adjudication legible.[12] Today, the one exercise of power that is clear is presidential decree—precisely the exercise of power the Constitution was designed to constrain.

For its part, speaking truth to conspiracy counteracts its corrosive force. What matters most is that officials with a connection to voters, with ties to concrete communities and social groups—in other words, elected officials—speak truth to conspiracy. Partisans trust fellow partisans more than they do reporters, professors, scientists, and unelected officials. The partisan connection needs to be two-directional: both a channel for citizens to transmit interests, views, and sentiments to government and one for officials to educate them and make government legible. The partisan connection is among the most important purposes of representation, if also among the most overlooked. It calls for speaking truth to conspiracy.

We see both responses to conspiracism at work. We see officials who insist on regular order and are determined to enact democracy. And we see some public officials—as well as the press, advocacy groups, civil society associations, and private citizens—determined to speak truth to conspiracy.

Future generations will judge us, no doubt, when it comes to democracy's will and capacity to provide a modicum of security and prosperity, to mitigate entrenched inequality, and to avoid catastrophe—to pull survival of the human habitat out from our careless destruction of the environment. Conspiracism is incapacitating and leads to political dysfunction; that is one reason to strike out against it. But will future generations care about democracy itself? Only if we resist the core conspiracist claim to own reality and its obliteration of common sense and a common political world. Democracy will retain its meaning and value only if citizens see it as the way to build that common world, and see their part in this project.

We echo the conspiracist in chief's warning: "There's something going on that's really, really bad. And we better get smart, and we better get tough, or we're not going to have much of a country left. O.K.?"[13] But we turn the warning back on itself. We are paying attention. We are smart enough to enact democracy, tough enough to speak truth to conspiracism. Our formidable political challenge is to recognize that "it is not enough, in this war of hoaxes and delusions and perpetuated lies, to be merely honest. It is necessary also to be wise."[14]

NOTES

Introduction

1. Michael Flynn was an unembarrassed spreader of conspiracism, including the charge that Hillary Clinton was a pedophile. See Timothy Snyder, *The Path to Unfreedom* (New York: Tim Duggan Books, 2018), 239.

2. The documents are likely to "help fuel a new generation of conspiracy theories," according to Philip Shenon, a former *New York Times* reporter, cited in Michael D. Shear, "Trump Says He Will Release Final Set of Documents on Kennedy Assassination," *New York Times*, October 21, 2017, https://www.nytimes.com/2017/10/21/us /politics/trump-jfk-assassination-classified.html.

3. Martin Parker, "Human Science as Conspiracy Theory," *Sociological Review* 48, no. 2 (October 2000): 191–207, 202. A recent example of conspiracy theorizing from the left is Nancy Maclean's *Democracy in Chains: The Deep History of the Radical Right's Stealth Plan for America* (New York: Viking, 2017), which uses documents and inference to shape a grand narrative: she attributes to public choice theorist James Buchanan, acting through Charles Koch, the "operational strategy" that made the Right successful over the last two decades, and attributes to Buchanan racist as well as conservative motives. For a scholarly assessment of the work, see Henry Farrell and Steven M. Teles, "When Politics Drives Scholarship," *Boston Review*, August 30, 2017, http://bostonreview.net/class-inequality/henry-farrell-steven-m-teles-when -politics-drives-scholarship.

4. Bruno Latour speaks of "those mad mixtures of knee-jerk disbelief, punctilious demands for proofs, and free use of powerful explanation from the social neverland" in *Politics of Nature: How to Bring the Sciences into Democracy* (Cambridge, MA: Harvard University Press, 2004), 230.

5. The FBI may well have been tapping Trump's phones, though Obama does not appear to have ordered it to have done so; see Eugene Kiely, "Revisiting Trump's Wiretap Tweets," FactCheck.org, September 22, 2017, https://www.factcheck.org/2017 /09/revisiting-trumps-wiretap-tweets/.

6. Christine Hauser, "Chobani Yoghurt Sues Alex Jones over Sexual Assault Report," *New York Times*, April 25, 2017, https://www.nytimes.com/2017/04/25 /business/chobani-alex-jones.html.

7. Dustin Tingley and Gernot Wagner, "Solar Geoengineering and the Chemtrails Conspiracy on Social Media," *Palgrave Communications* 3 (2017): article 12, https://

doi.org/10.1057/s41599-017-0014-3. "Chemtrails are not real," according to the Environmental Protection Agency and scientists; the trails are water vapor, the product of jet engines. Meanwhile, 2016 polling cited shows that 10 percent think the conspiracy is "completely true" and another 20–30 percent describe it as "somewhat true."

8. Jeremy W. Peters, "The Right Builds an Alternative Narrative about the Crises around Trump," *New York Times*, May 17, 2017, https://www.nytimes.com/2017/05/17/us/politics/trump-scandal-conservatives-media.html.

9. As David Runciman points out in *How Democracy Ends* (New York: Basic Books, 2018), 20.

10. Polling suggests that conspiracism is indeed widespread: "Conspiracy theories permeate all parts of American society, and cut across gender, age, race, income, political affiliation, educational level, and occupational status." So, for example, about a third of Americans believe the birther conspiracy theory that President Obama is not a native-born American but rather a Kenyan, cited in Joseph E. Uscinski and Joseph M. Parent, *American Conspiracy Theories* (Oxford: Oxford University Press, 2014), 5. Another study found that "while some people hold mostly crazy beliefs, most people hold at least some crazy beliefs." Adam J. Berinsky, "Rumors, Truths, and Reality: A Study of Political Misinformation" (unpublished manuscript, May 22, 2012, version 3.1 on file with the authors), http://web.mit.edu/berinsky/www/files/rumor.pdf. See also the Chapman University Survey of American Fears, wave 3 (2016), in which 75 percent of respondents stated that they believed the government is concealing information about at least one of the nine conspiracy theories the poll inquired about; "What Aren't They Telling Us, Chapman University Survey of American Fears," Chapman University, Wilkinson College of Arts, Humanities, and Social Sciences, October 11, 2016, https://blogs.chapman.edu/wilkinson/2016/10/11/what-arent-they-telling-us/.

11. J. Eric Oliver and Thomas J. Wood, "Conspiracy Theories and the Paranoid Style(s) of Mass Opinion," *American Journal of Political Science* 58, no. 2 (October 2014): 952–66, 953.

12. John Dewey quoted in Jill Lepore, "The World That Trump and Ailes Built," *New Yorker*, June 5 and 12, 2017, https://www.newyorker.com/magazine/2017/06/05/the-world-that-trump-and-ailes-built.

13. For a detailed timeline of events, see "Flint Water Crisis Fast Facts," CNN, last updated April 8, 2018, https://www.cnn.com/2016/03/04/us/flint-water-crisis-fast-facts/index.html. A good overview is Anna Marie Barry-Jester, "What Went Wrong in Flint?," FiveThirtyEight, January 26, 2016, https://fivethirtyeight.com/features/what-went-wrong-in-flint-water-crisis-michigan/.

14. Mark Fenster, *Conspiracy Theories: Secrecy and Power in American Culture* (Minneapolis: University of Minnesota Press, 1999), xv.

15. Jonathan Mahler, "What Do We Really Know about Osama Bin Laden's Death?," *New York Times*, October 15, 2015, https://www.nytimes.com/2015/10/18/magazine/what-do-we-really-know-about-osama-bin-ladens-death.html.

16. Steven M. Smallpage, Adam M. Enders, and Joseph E. Uscinski, "The Partisan Contours of Conspiracy Theory Beliefs," *Research and Politics* 4, no. 4 (October

2017), online version published December 11, 2017, https://doi.org/10.1177 /2053168017746554.

17. Runciman, *How Democracy Ends*, 64.

18. For the full text of the indictment, see "Text: Full Mueller Indictment on Russian Election Case," Politico, February 16, 2018, https://www.politico.com/story/2018 /02/16/text-full-mueller-indictment-on-russian-election-case-415670.

19. Rebecca Morin, "Bolton: Russian Hacks Could Actually Have Been by Obama Administration," Politico, December 11, 2016, https://www.politico.com/story/2016 /12/john-bolton-russia-hack-a-false-flag-232490.

20. Samantha Schmidt, "A Coup in America? Fox News Escalates Anti-Mueller Rhetoric," *Washington Post*, December 18, 2017, https://www.washingtonpost.com /news/morning-mix/wp/2017/12/18/a-coup-in-america-fox-news-escalates-anti -mueller-rhetoric.

21. David Runciman addressed this question and the relation to skepticism in his lecture "Are Conspiracy Theories Bad for Democracy?" (London School of Economics, February 10, 2016), http://www.lse.ac.uk/Events/2016/02/20160210t1830vHKT /Are-Conspiracy-Theories-Bad-for-Democracy.

22. For example, the rumor that, as a result of the Trump administration's "zero-tolerance" policy and the forcible separation of migrant children from their families, the government had "lost" 1,500 children. The data were from 2014 under different circumstances; though the claim was repeated widely, it was quickly corrected and those who had repeated it, like Senator Ed Markey, Democrat from Massachusetts, retracted the charge. A. J. Willingham, "Here's What's Really Happening with the 1,500 'Missing' Immigrant Children," CNN, last updated May 29, 2018, https://www.cnn .com/2018/05/29/us/immigration-refugee-child-missing-hhs-obama-photo-trnd /index.html; McKay Coppins, "How the Left Lost Its Mind," *Atlantic*, July 2, 2017, https://www.theatlantic.com/politics/archive/2017/07/liberal-fever-swamps /530736/.

23. Pierre Rosanvallon, *Good Government: Democracy beyond Elections*, trans. Malcolm DeBevoise (Cambridge, MA: Harvard University Press, 2018), 146–71.

24. Max Weber, "Politics as a Vocation," in *The Vocation Lectures* (Indianapolis: Hackett, 2004).

25. In related studies, political scientists discuss threats to democracy. For example, Steven Levitsky and Daniel Ziblatt identify four warning signs of the turn to authoritarianism: the leader shows only a weak commitment to democratic rules, denies the legitimacy of opponents, tolerates or encourages violence, and shows some willingness to curb civil liberties or the media; Steven Levitsky and Daniel Ziblatt, *How Democracies Die* (New York: Crown, 2018), 23–24.

Chapter 1. Conspiracy without the Theory

1. Martin Parker, "Human Science as Conspiracy Theory," *Sociological Review* 48, no. 2 (October 2000): 191–207, 202.

2. Architects and Engineers for 9/11 Truth website, accessed September 13, 2018, https://www.ae911truth.org/.

3. For a thorough analysis of 9/11 conspiracy theories, see Charles B. Strozier, "Historical Perspectives on the 9/11 Conspiracy Movement," 2010 (unpublished essay on file with the authors). Also see the Complete 911 Timeline Investigative Project hosted by History Commons, accessed September 13, 2018, http://www.historycommons.org/project.jsp?project=911_project.

4. Brian L. Keeley, "Of Conspiracy Theories," *Journal of Philosophy* 96, no. 3 (March 1999): 109–26, 117.

5. History belies the "all men," of course, and there is an enormous literature on which of the founders thought what about African and Native Americans, women, and many classes of Caucasian European men.

6. Bernard Bailyn, *The Ideological Origins of the American Revolution* (Cambridge, MA: Harvard University Press, 1967), 95.

7. Bailyn, *Ideological Origins*, 94–95.

8. Gordon Wood, "Conspiracy and the Paranoid Style: Causality and Deceit in the Eighteenth Century," *William and Mary Quarterly* 39, no. 3 (July 1982): 401–41, 421. Wood documents the change from a framework that understands causality in terms of individual moral agency with an emphasis on intentions to one that emphasizes general social processes, such as the market's "invisible hand" and unintended consequences. Because conspiracy theories reflect the earlier notion of causality, they are often dubbed irrational, not quite normal, and "paranoid."

9. David Brion Davis, *Fear of Conspiracy: Images of Un-American Subversion from the Revolution to the Present* (Ithaca, NY: Cornell University Press, 2008), 24–25.

10. Alexander Hamilton, *The Farmer Refuted*, quoted in Eric Nelson, "What Kind of Book Is *The Ideological Origins of the American Revolution*?," *New England Quarterly* 90, no. 1 (March 2018): 147–71, 167.

11. Nelson, 158.

12. Bailyn, *Ideological Origins*, 95.

13. Pauline Maier, *American Scripture: Making the Declaration of Independence* (New York: Vintage, 1998).

14. Sonam Sheth, "NPR Tweeted Out the Declaration of Independence on July 4—and Twitter Went Nuts," *Business Insider*, June 5, 2017, http://www.businessinsider.com/trump-supporters-react-to-npr-declaration-of-independence-tweets-2017-7.

15. Davis, *Fear of Conspiracy*, 23.

16. Brian L. Keeley, "On Conspiracy Theories," *Journal of Philosophy* 96, no. 3 (March 1999): 109–26, 116.

17. Keeley, 116.

18. Isaac Stanley-Becker, "'We Are Q': A Deranged Conspiracy Cult Leaps from the Internet to the Crowd at Trump's 'MAGA' Tour," *Washington Post*, August 1, 2018, http://www.washingtonpost.com/news/morning-mix/wp/2018/08; Paris Martineau, "The Storm Is the New Pizzagate—Only Worse," *New York*, December 19, 2017, http://nymag.com/selectall/2017/12/qanon-4chan-the-storm-conspiracy-explained.html.

19. Lena H. Sun and Sari Horwitz, "Conspiracy Theories Swirl around the Death of Antonin Scalia," *Washington Post*, February 15, 2016, https://www.washingtonpost.com/news/post-nation/wp/2016/02/15/conspiracy-theories-swirl-around-the-death-of-antonin-scalia/?utm_term=.5a656535f0c2.

20. Rob Brotherton, *Suspicious Minds: Why We Believe Conspiracy Theories* (London: Bloomsbury Sigma, 2015), 78.

21. Glenn Thrush and Maggie Haberman, "Trump Aides Address His Wiretap Claims: 'That's above My Pay Grade,'" *New York Times*, March 7, 2017, https://www.nytimes.com/2017/03/07/us/politics/trump-wiretap-claim-obama.html.

22. Bryan Clark, "Rep Shares Article Saying Charlottesville Was 'Set-Up,'" *Idaho Post Register*, August 18, 2017, http://www.spokesman.com/stories/2017/aug/18/idaho-state-rep-shares-article-saying-charlottesvi/.

23. Delegitimation is also what Steve Bannon, no standard Republican, went after openly and ferociously when he advocated "deconstruction of the administrative state." Philip Rucker and Robert Costa, "Bannon Vows a Daily Fight for 'Deconstruction of the Administrative State,'" *Washington Post*, February 23, 2017, https://www.washingtonpost.com/politics/top-wh-strategist-vows-a-daily-fight-for-deconstruction-of-the-administrative-state/2017/02/23/03f6b8da-f9ea-11e6-bf01-d47f8cf9b643_story.html?utm_term=.f07737a77bb0.

24. Richard Hofstadter, *The Paranoid Style in America Politics and Other Essays* (Cambridge, MA: Harvard University Press, 1964), 29.

25. Nelson, "What Kind of Book?," 163.

26. Ivan Krastev, "The Rise of the Paranoid Citizen," *New York Times*, March 16, 2017, https://www.nytimes.com/2017/03/16/opinion/the-rise-of-the-paranoid-citizen.html.

27. Jay Ogilvy, "The Apocalyptic Vision of Stephen K. Bannon," *Forbes*, August 17, 2017, https://www.forbes.com/sites/stratfor/2017/08/17/the-apocalyptic-vision-of-stephen-k-bannon/.

28. Faiz Siddiqui and Susan Svrluga, "N.C. Man Told Police He Went to D.C. Pizzeria with Gun to Investigate Conspiracy Theory," *Washington Post*, December 5, 2016, https://www.washingtonpost.com/news/local/wp/2016/12/04/d-c-police-respond-to-report-of-a-man-with-a-gun-at-comet-ping-pong-restaurant/?utm_term=.0ffba0f83aec. On Russian contributions to the Pizzagate narrative, see Timothy Snyder, *The Road to Unfreedom* (New York: Tim Duggan Books, 2018), 246.

29. Krastev, "Rise of the Paranoid Citizen."

30. "Transcript: ABC News Anchor David Muir Interviews President Trump," *ABC News*, January 25, 2017, http://abcnews.go.com/Politics/transcript-abc-news-anchor-david-muir-interviews-president/story?id=45047602.

31. Snyder, *Road to Unfreedom*, 229.

32. Jonathan Albright, an assistant professor of media analytics at Elon University in North Carolina, quoted in "Belleville Woman Helped Cook Up Pizzagate," *Star* (Toronto), December 7, 2016, https://www.thestar.com/news/canada/2016/12/07/belleville-woman-helped-cook-up-pizzagate.html. When these bots were part of the

Russian campaign to influence the presidential election, ordinary people who spread them become unwitting accomplices in a foreign hacking operation; see Snyder, *Road to Unfreedom*, 228–231.

33. Karen S. Cook, Margaret Levi, and Russell Hardin, *Whom Can We Trust: How Groups, Networks, and Institutions Make Trust Possible* (New York: Russell Sage Foundation, 2009), 1.

34. Abigail Tracy, "Republicans Say Firing Mueller Is the Only Way to Prevent a 'Coup,'" *Vanity Fair*, November 9, 2017, https://www.vanityfair.com/news/2017/11/republicans-robert-mueller-russia-investigation.

35. Samantha Schmidt, "A 'Coup in America'? Fox News Escalates Anti-Mueller Rhetoric," *Washington Post*, December 18, 2017, https://www.washingtonpost.com/news/morning-mix/wp/2017/12/18/a-coup-in-america-fox-news-escalates-anti-mueller-rhetoric/.

36. Emily Stewart, "Fox News's FBI Coup Conspiracy Theory, Explained," *Vox*, December 18, 2017, https://www.vox.com/policy-and-politics/2017/12/18/16790592/fox-news-coup.

37. Snyder, *Road to Unfreedom*, 232.

38. The point is made by Brotherton, *Suspicious Minds*, 68.

39. Brotherton, 78.

40. Glenn Kessler, "Huckabee's 'Kenya' Clarification Also Raises More Questions," *Washington Post*, March 2, 2011, http://voices.washingtonpost.com/fact-checker/2011/03/huckabees_kenya_clarification.html. Also see Jennifer L. Hochschild and Katherine Levine Einstein, *Do Facts Matter? Information and Misinformation in American Politics* (Norman: University of Oklahoma Press, 2015), 108–9.

41. Ronald Reagan, "Inauguration Address," January 20, 1981, Avalon Project: Documents in Law, History, and Diplomacy, Yale Law School, http://avalon.law.yale.edu/20th_century/reagan1.asp.

Chapter 2. It's True Enough

1. Glenn Thrush and Maggie Haberman, "Trump Aides Address His Wiretap Claims: 'That's above My Pay Grade,'" *New York Times*, March 7, 2017, https://www.nytimes.com/2017/03/07/us/politics/trump-wiretap-claim-obama.html.

2. Bryan Clark, "Rep Shares Article Saying Charlottesville Was 'Set-Up,'" *Idaho Post Register*, August 18, 2017, http://www.spokesman.com/stories/2017/aug/18/idaho-state-rep-shares-article-saying-charlottesvi/.

3. Cass R. Sunstein and Adrian Vermeule, "Conspiracy Theories: Causes and Cures," *Journal of Political Philosophy* 17, no. 2 (2009): 202–27, 204.

4. Richard Hofstadter, *The Paranoid Style in American Politics and Other Essays* (Cambridge, MA: Harvard University Press, 1964), 5.

5. Hofstadter noted that his case studies, covering topics ranging from the Bavarian illuminati to anti-Communists in the 1950s, focused on minority movements and marginal elements in American society; *Paranoid Style*, 10.

6. Hofstadter, 31.

7. Hofstadter, 4.

8. See, for example, Joseph E. Uscinski and Joseph M. Parent, *American Conspiracy Theories* (Oxford: Oxford University Press, 2014), 154.

9. Brian L. Keeley, "Of Conspiracy Theories," *Journal of Philosophy* 96, no. 3 (March 1999): 109–26, 124.

10. Quoted in Hofstadter, *Paranoid Style*, 7.

11. Keeley, "Of Conspiracy Theories," 124.

12. Hofstadter, *Paranoid Style*, 36.

13. Eli Yokley, "Many Republicans Doubt Clinton Won the Popular Vote," Morning Consult, July 26, 2017, https://morningconsult.com/2017/07/26/many -republicans-think-trump-won-2016-popular-vote-didnt/.

14. Adam J. Berinsky, "Rumors, Truths, and Reality: A Study of Political Misinformation" (unpublished manuscript, May 22, 2012, version 3.1), accessed September 27, 2018, http://web.mit.edu/berinsky/www/files/rumor.pdf.

15. Uscinski and Parent, *American Conspiracy Theories*, 90–91.

16. Brendan Nyhan, "Why More Democrats Are Now Embracing Conspiracy Theories," *New York Times*, February 15, 2017, https://www.nytimes.com/2017/02 /15/upshot/why-more-democrats-are-now-embracing-conspiracy-theories.html.

17. Uscinski and Parent, *American Conspiracy Theories*, 151.

18. Brendan Nyhan and Jason Reifler, "When Corrections Fail: The Persistence of Political Misperceptions," *Political Behavior* 32, no. 2 (June 2010): 303–30.

19. Chris Cillizza, "Donald Trump Still Has No Evidence That His Wiretapping Claim Was Right," CNN, September 19, 2018, https://www.cnn.com/2017/09/19 /politics/trump-wiretapping-manafort/index.html.

20. Berinsky, "Rumors, Truths, and Reality," 15.

21. Peter Knight, "Outrageous Conspiracy Theories: Popular and Official Responses to 9/11 in Germany and the United States," *New German Critique* 103, no. 1 (Spring 2008): 165–93, 165.

22. Morning Consult/Politico poll, cited in Steven Levitsky and Daniel Ziblatt, *How Democracies Die* (New York: Crown, 2018), 197.

23. Uscinski and Parent, *American Conspiracy Theories*, 130–53.

24. Some philosophers would argue that all beliefs rest on a kind of true-enoughness, or verisimilitude. In this view, we never validate our beliefs to the point of perfect certainty; we can only attempt to falsify them, and beliefs that have stood the test of falsification are corroborated. Yet even so, they might be falsified in the future, which is why we cannot have perfect certainty in them: our beliefs have a verisimilitude or truth-likeness when they survive falsification tests, even if we cannot say for sure that they are true. True-enoughness as we see it, by contrast, is not subject to any falsification test. If it seems possible, it satisfies the true-enough test. See Karl R. Popper, *The Logic of Scientific Discovery* (London: Hutchinson, 1959).

25. Daniel A. Effron, "Why Trump Supporters Don't Mind His Lies," *New York Times*, April 28, 2018, https://www.nytimes.com/2018/04/28/opinion/sunday/why -trump-supporters-dont-mind-his-lies.html.

26. Adam Berinsky argues that the degree to which people assent to propositions they know are factually inaccurate (because they derive expressive satisfaction from the act of assent) is very small. His study only tested for respondents who express beliefs that contradict what they genuinely believe—for instance, those who believe Obama was born in the US but derive expressive satisfaction from saying he was born in Kenya. Our focus is different: that people are motivated by tribal loyalties. We are not claiming that they are motivated by tribal loyalties to affirm things they know are incorrect—we accept Berinsky's findings. It is consistent with these findings to hold that people both assent to and believe conspiracist claims because they seem true enough. See Adam J. Berinsky, "Telling the Truth about Believing the Lies? Evidence for the Limited Prevalence of Expressive Survey Responding," *Journal of Politics* 80, no. 1, published online October 26, 2017, https://doi.org/10.1086/694258.

27. A steady stream of research finds a link between conspiracy thinking and party attachment. Even without agreement on the dynamic, this finding remains strong. See Joseph E. Uscinski and Santiago Olivella, "The Conditional Effect of Conspiracy Thinking on Attitudes toward Climate Change," *Research and Politics* 4, no. 4 (October 2017): 1–9. Brendan Nyhan adds to partisanship whether the party is in or out of power: "Why More Democrats Are Now Embracing Conspiracy Theories," *The Upshot, New York Times*, February 15, 2017, https://www.nytimes.com/2017/02/15/upshot/why-more-democrats-are-now-embracing-conspiracy-theories.html.

28. Kathy Francovic, "Belief in Conspiracies Largely Depends on Political Identity," YouGov poll, December 26, 2016, https://today.yougov.com/news/2016/12/27/belief-conspiracies-largely-depends-political-iden/.

29. Julia Glum, "Some Republicans Still Think Obama Was Born in Kenya as Trump Resurrects Birther Conspiracy Theory," *Newsweek*, December 11, 2017, http://www.newsweek.com/trump-birther-obama-poll-republicans-kenya-744195.

30. Kate Starbird, "Information Wars: A Window into the Alternative Media Ecosystem," Medium, March 14, 2017, https://medium.com/hci-design-at-uw/information-wars-a-window-into-the-alternative-media-ecosystem-a1347f32fd8f.

31. Jerome Bruner, "The Narrative Construction of Reality," *Critical Inquiry* 18 (Autumn 1991): 1–20.

32. Robert Jay Lifton on Bruner in "The Assault on Reality," *Dissent*, April 10, 2018, https://www.dissentmagazine.org/online_articles/assault-on-reality-robert-lifton-trump.

33. Michael Hiltzik, "Stephen Glass Is Still Retracting His Fabricated Stories—18 Years Later," *Los Angeles Times*, December 15, 2015, http://www.latimes.com/business/hiltzik/la-fi-mh-stephen-glass-is-still-retracting-20151215-column.html.

34. Cited in Thomas B. Edsall, "Democracy Can Plant the Seeds of Its Own Destruction," *New York Times*, October 19, 2017, https://www.nytimes.com/2017/10/19/opinion/democracy-populism-trump.html.

35. PolitiFact (@PolitiFact), "Trump said, 'Some people say (Michael Flynn) lied and some people say he didn't lie. I mean, really, it turned out maybe he didn't lie.'

This isn't in question," Twitter, June 15, 2018, 11:12 a.m., https://twitter.com/politifact /status/1007687181266243585; Jon Greenberg et al., "Fact-Checking Donald Trump's Interviews with Fox and Friends, Reporters on the White House Lawn," PolitiFact, June 15, 2018, http://www.politifact.com/truth-o-meter/article/2018/jun/15/fact -checking-donald-trumps-unusual-white-house-la/.

36. Michiko Kakutani, *The Death of Truth: Notes on Falsehood in the Age of Trump* (New York: Tim Duggan Books, 2018), 29.

37. "Your reputation is amazing . . . I will not let you down," Trump told Jones, as quoted in Matt Ford, "The Legal War on Alex Jones," *New Republic*, May 29, 2018, https://newrepublic.com/article/148562/legal-war-on-alex-jones.

38. Ford.

39. David Montero, "Jones Settles Chobani Lawsuit and Retracts Comments about Refugees in Twin Falls, Idaho," *Los Angeles Times*, May 17, 2017, http://www.latimes .com/nation/la-na-chobani-alex-jones-20170517-story.html; Mallory Shelbourne, "In-fowars' Alex Jones Apologizes for Pushing 'Pizzagate' Conspiracy Theory," *Hill*, March 25, 2017, https://thehill.com/homenews/325761-infowars-alex-jones-apologizes -for-pushing-pizzagate-conspiracy-theory.

40. "Belleville Woman Helped Cook Up Pizzagate," *Star* (Toronto), December 7, 2016, https://www.thestar.com/news/canada/2016/12/07/belleville-woman-helped -cook-up-pizzagate.html.

41. Michael M. Gryngaum, "Right-Wing Media Uses Parkland Shooting as Con-spiracy Fodder," *New York Times*, February 20, 2018, https://www.nytimes.com/2018 /02/20/business/media/parkland-shooting-media-conspiracy.html.

42. Michelle Ye Hee Lee, "Donald Trump's False Comments Connecting Mexican Immigrants and Crime," *Washington Post*, July 8, 2015, https://www.washingtonpost .com/news/fact-checker/wp/2015/07/08/donald-trumps-false-comments -connecting-mexican-immigrants-and-crime/.

43. *Oxford English Dictionary Online*, s.v. "scapegoat," http://www.oed.com/view /Entry/171946.

44. Mark Fenster, *Conspiracy Theories: Secrecy and Power in American Culture*, (Minneapolis, MN: University of Minnesota Press, 2008), 89.

45. Donald J. Trump (@realDonaldTrump), Twitter, June 19, 2018, 6:52 a.m., https://twitter.com/realdonaldtrump/status/1009071403918864385?lang=en.

Chapter 3. Presidential Conspiracism

1. Jeffrey Tulis, *The Rhetorical Presidency*, new ed. with afterword by the author (Princeton, NJ: Princeton University Press, 2017).

2. Tulis, 203.

3. James Madison, *Federalist*, no. 10, November 23, 1787, https://www.congress .gov/resources/display/content/The+Federalist+Papers#TheFederalistPapers-10.

4. John Jay, *Federalist*, no. 2, October 31, 1787, https://www.congress.gov /resources/display/content/The+Federalist+Papers#TheFederalistPapers-2.

5. "Transcript, Illinois Senate Candidate Barack Obama," *Washington Post*, July 27, 2004, http://www.washingtonpost.com/wp-dyn/articles/A19751-2004Jul27.html.

6. "Here's Donald Trump's Presidential Announcement Speech," *Time*, June 16, 2015, http://time.com/3923128/donald-trump-announcement-speech/.

7. Inis Novacic, "Muslim Enclave in U.S. Battles Suspicion, Alleged Threats," CBS News, July 16, 2015, http://www.cbsnews.com/news/inside-islamberg/.

8. Jenna Johnson, "Trump Doesn't Correct Rally Attendee Who Says Obama Is a Muslim and Not Even an American," *Washington Post*, September 17, 2015, https://www.washingtonpost.com/news/post-politics/wp/2015/09/17/trump-doesnt-correct-rally-attendee-who-says-obama-is-muslim-and-not-even-an-american/.

9. C. K. Williams, "Bishop Tutu's Visit to the White House: 1984," in *Selected Poems* (New York: Farrar, Straus, and Giroux, 1994), 133.

10. Daren Butler and Orhan Coskon, "Turkish Troops Hunt Remaining Coup Plotters as Crackdown Widens," Reuters, July 26, 2016, https://www.reuters.com/article/us-turkey-security-idUSKCN1061DK.

11. After the referendum, suspicious about negotiations over leaving the European Union, Brexit supporters turn conspiracist: George Soros (Jewish money) is working to overturn the referendum results and "to flood Christian Europe with Muslim refugees." See "Brexiters Now March with the Toxic Conspiracies of Orban's Hungary," *Guardian*, February 10, 2018, https://www.theguardian.com/commentisfree/2018/feb/10/brexiters-now-march-with-toxic-conspirators-of-orbans-hungary.

12. We speak of populism as a *political style* in this context because Trump's policies—with the exception of his border wall and a few other items—are those of conservative Republicans. We call this the "partisan penumbra," the subject of chapter 4. Populist policy typically consists of protection from the foreign: protecting the country from immigrants via extreme measures ("Build the wall!") and nativist clamor for protection from foreign competition that hurts workers ("End NAFTA!"). Trump adheres to these positions, at least rhetorically. But one might ask whether policies that advantage the 1 percent, harm the middle class, and erode the safety net of the least well off are genuinely populist.

13. Jan-Werner Müeller, "The Majority of Deplorables?," Project Syndicate, November 10, 2016, https://www.project-syndicate.org/commentary/trump-voters-opposition-to-democracy-by-jan-werner-mueller-2016-11; Yascha Mounk, *The People vs. Democracy* (Cambridge, MA: Harvard University Press, 2018).

14. Jan-Werner Müller, *What Is Populism?* (Philadelphia: University of Pennsylvania Press, 2016), 10. The quote from Rosenblum is on p. 20.

15. William Galston, *Anti-pluralism: The Populist Threat to Liberal Democracy* (New Haven, CT: Yale University Press, 2018).

16. Nadia Urbinati, *Democracy Disfigured: Opinion, Truth, and the People* (Cambridge, MA: Harvard University Press, 2014), 130–35; Nadia Urbinati, "Populism and the Principle of Majority," in *The Oxford Handbook on Pluralism*, ed. Cristóbal Rovira Kaltwasser et al. (New York: Oxford University Press, 2017).

17. Haley Muse, "Jake Tapper Lists Conspiracy Theories Spread by Trump," CNN, May 23, 2018, https://www.cnn.com/2018/05/23/politics/jake-tapper-trump-conspiracy-theories-special-counsel-cnntv/index.html; Maggie Haberman, "Even as He Rises, Donald Trump Entertains Conspiracy Theories," *New York Times*, February 29, 2016, https://www.nytimes.com/2016/03/01/us/politics/donald-trump-conspiracy-theories.html.

18. Adam Entous and Ronan Farrow, "The Conspiracy Memo about Obama Aides That Circulated in the Trump White House," *New Yorker*, August 23, 2018, https://www.newyorker.com/news/news-desk/the-conspiracy-memo-aimed-at-obama-aides-that-circulated-in-the-trump-white-house.

19. Julie Hirschfield Davis and Maggie Haberman, "After Vowing to Fix Washington, Trump Is Mired in a Familiar Crisis," *New York Times*, January 20, 2018, https://www.nytimes.com/2018/01/20/us/politics/trump-shutdown.html.

20. Louis Jacobson, "In Context: Donald Trump's 'Second Amendment People' Comment," PolitiFact, August 9, 2016, http://www.politifact.com/truth-o-meter/article/2016/aug/09/context-donald-trumps-second-amendment-people-comm/.

21. Conversation with talk show host Joe Scarborough as reported in Michael Wolff, *Fire and Fury: Inside the Trump White House* (New York: Henry Holt, 2018), 47.

22. Quoted in Charles Blow, "In Defense of Truth," *New York Times*, September 4, 2017, https://www.nytimes.com/2017/09/04/opinion/trump-truth-wiretapping-obama.html.

23. Peter Baker and Eileen Sullivan, "Trump Has a Few Things He'd Like to Get off His Chest," *New York Times*, June 15, 2018, https://www.nytimes.com/2018/06/15/us/politics/trump-fbi-democrats-obama.html.

24. Greg Kessler, Salvador Rizzo, and Meg Kelly, "President Trump Has Made 3001 False or Misleading Claims So Far," *Washington Post*, May 1, 2018, https://www.washingtonpost.com/news/fact-checker/wp/2018/05/01/president-trump-has-made-3001-false-or-misleading-claims-so-far/?utm_term=.c0109235a6dd; Daniel Dale, "Donald Trump Makes 21 False Claims in Missouri Speech on Tax Plan," *Star* (Toronto), December 7, 2017, https://www.thestar.com/news/0world/analysis/2017/11/28/daniel-dales-donald-trump-fact-check-updates.html.

25. The *Washington Post*'s Fact Checker report cited in Charles Blow, "What Doesn't Kill Him Makes Him Stronger," *New York Times*, July 25, 2018, https://www.nytimes.com/2018/07/25/opinion/donald-trump-facts-lies.htm.

26. Vaclav Havel, "The Power of the Powerless," in *The Power of the Powerless*, intro. by Steven Lukes, ed. John Keane (New York: Routledge, 2015), 27.

27. Harry G. Frankfurt, *On Bullshit* (Princeton, NJ: Princeton University Press, 2005).

28. Hannah Arendt, "Truth and Politics," in *Between Past and Future*, rev. ed. (New York: Penguin Classics, 2006), 234.

29. Robert Jay Lifton, *The Climate Swerve: Reflections on Mind, Hope, and Survival* (New York: New Press, 2017), 67–70.

30. Peter Baker and Maggie Haberman, "A Conspiracy Theory's Journey from Talk Radio to Trump's Twitter," *New York Times*, March 5, 2017, https://www.nytimes.com /2017/03/05/us/politics/trump-twitter-talk-radio-conspiracy-theory.html.

31. Jim Sciutto and Mary Kay Mallonee, "CIA Director Met with DNC Hack Conspiracy Theorist at Trump's Urging," CNN, November 8, 2017, https://www.cnn.com /2017/11/07/politics/mike-pompeo-william-binney-meeting/index.html.

32. "Why Has Kris Kobach's Voter Fraud Commission Disappeared?," editorial, *Kansas City Star*, November 1, 2017, http://www.kansascity.com/opinion/editorials /article182150656.html.

33. Lee Moran, "Seth Meyers Tears into Donald Trump's 'Crazy' Tweets during James Comey Hearing," *Huffington Post*, March 21, 2017, http://www.huffingtonpost .com/entry/seth-meyers-donald-trump-comey-hearing_us_58d0d371e4b0ec 9d29ded0ce?.

34. Thomas Friedman, "Peanut Butter on the Trump Team's Chins," *New York Times*, March 7, 2017, https://www.nytimes.com/2017/03/07/opinion/peanut-butter -on-the-trump-teams-chins.html.

35. Joshua Green, *Devil's Bargain: Steve Bannon, Donald Trump, and the Storming of the Presidency* (New York: Penguin, 2017), 38.

36. Green, 190.

37. Peter Baker, "Bound to No Party, Trump Upends 150 Years of Two-Party Rule," *New York Times*, September 9, 2017, https://www.nytimes.com/2017/09/09/us /politics/trump-republicans-third-parties.html.

38. Susan B. Glasser, "The GOPs Civil War over Trump," *Politico Magazine*, August 14, 2017, https://www.politico.com/magazine/story/2017/08/14/donald-trump -future-of-gop-roundtable-215485.

39. Green, *Devil's Bargain*, 169.

40. Sheryl Gay Stolberg, "Trump Republicans Invigorate, and Complicate, Party's Fight for Senate," *New York Times*, August 29, 2017, https://www.nytimes.com/2017 /08/29/us/politics/senate-trump-lou-barletta-.html?mtrref=www.google.com&gwh =A71A1C2523EB0B9C3BFF4F8728F7C20E&gwt=pay.

41. Mike DeBonis and Josh Wagner, "House Rejects Immigration Bill Pushed by Trump in Last-Minute Tweet," *Washington Post*, June 27, 2018, https://www .washingtonpost.com/politics/trump-using-all-caps-in-a-tweet-urges-passage-of-the -house-gop-immigration-bill/2018/06/27/989b2ad8-7960-11e8-80be-6d32e182a3bc _story.html?utm_term=.92adc52f3cd2.

42. Charles Blow, "Rise of the Roypublicans," *New York Times*, December 10, 2017, https://www.nytimes.com/2017/12/10/opinion/republicans-roy-moore -harassment.html.

Chapter 4. Political Parties

1. Pierre Rosanvallon, *Democratic Legitimacy: Impartiality, Reflexivity, Proximity*, trans. Arthur Goldhammer (Princeton, NJ: Princeton University Press, 2011), 163;

Rosanvallon's focus, in addition to administration, is oversight by constitutional courts. For an empirical account of the American pendulum swing between popular democracy and administration, see Bruce Cain, *Democracy More or Less: America's Political Reform Quandary* (Cambridge: Cambridge University Press, 2015). Many theorists of democracy recognize just one of these institutions as foundational: political representation. The questions that propel their work have to do with the justification and design of institutions where conflicting interests and values are expressed, deliberated, and resolved. Few focus on the administrative state or what is variously called bureaucracy or technocracy.

2. Nadia Urbinati, *Democracy Disfigured: Opinion, Truth, and the People* (Cambridge, MA: Harvard University Press, 2014).

3. Russell Muirhead and Nancy L. Rosenblum, "The Partisan Connection," *California Law Review Circuit* 3 (March 2012): 99–102.

4. Judith Shklar, *American Citizenship: The Quest for Inclusion* (Cambridge, MA: Harvard University Press, 1991), 25.

5. Nancy L. Rosenblum, *On the Side of the Angels: An Appreciation of Parties and Partisanship* (Princeton, NJ: Princeton University Press, 2008).

6. Maurice Duverger, *Political Parties* (New York: Routledge and Kegan Paul, 1964).

7. See, for example, Bruce Ackerman, *We the People* (Cambridge, MA: Harvard University Press, 1991); and Edward Carmines and James Stimson, *Issue Evolution* (Princeton, NJ: Princeton University Press, 1989).

8. Mark Lander, "Trump Accuses Democrats of 'Treason' amid Market Rout," *New York Times*, February 5, 2018, https://www.nytimes.com/2018/02/05/us/politics/trump-accuses-democrats-treason-market-rout.html.

9. Brandon Carter, "Huckabee Sanders: Dems Need to Decide Whether They 'Hate' Trump 'More than They Love This Country,'" *Hill*, February 6, 2018, http://thehill.com/homenews/administration/372615-huckabee-sanders-dems-need-to-decide-if-they-hate-trump-more-than.

10. Moises Velasquez-Manoff, "Trump Ruins Irony, Too," *New York Times*, March 20, 2017, https://www.nytimes.com/2017/03/20/opinion/trump-ruins-irony-too.html.

11. Tim Carpenter, "Kansas Panel Delays Ballot Decision on Obama," *Topeka Capital-Journal*, September 13, 2012, http://www.cjonline.com/2016-04-05/stub-2060.

12. Joshua Green, *Devil's Bargain: Steve Bannon, Donald Trump, and the Storming of the Presidency* (New York: Penguin, 2017), 9.

13. Michael D. Shear, "If G.O.P. Loses Hold on Congress, Trump Warns, Democrats Will Enact Change 'Quickly and Violently,'" *New York Times*, August 28, 2018, https://www.nytimes.com/2018/08/28/us/politics/trump-evangelical-pastors-election.html.

14. Adam Liptak and Michael D. Shear, "Supreme Court Weighs Obama's Immigration Plan," *New York Times*, April 18, 2016, https://www.nytimes.com/2016/04/19/us/politics/supreme-court-immigration.html?hp&action=click&pgtype=Homepage&clickSource=story-heading&module=first-column-region&region=top-news&WT.nav=top-news.

15. Jennifer Steinhauer, "Mitch McConnell's Stance in Confirmation Fight Could Help and Hurt GOP," *New York Times*, February 14, 2016, https://www.nytimes.com /2016/02/15/us/politics/mitch-mcconnells-stance-in-confirmation-fight-could -help-and-hurt-gop.html.

16. Norman Ornstein and Thomas E. Mann, "The Threat of Bush's Signing Statements," op-ed, Brookings Institute, July 7, 2006, https://www.brookings.edu/opinions /the-threat-of-bushs-signing-statements/.

17. Green, *Devil's Bargain*, 222.

18. "Transcript of the N.H. GOP Debate, Annotated," *Washington Post*, February 6, 2018, https://www.washingtonpost.com/news/the-fix/wp/2016/02/06/transcript-of -the-feb-6-gop-debate-annotated/?utm_term=.bf8eadaf400e.

19. Green, *Devil's Bargain*, 8.

20. Frank J. Sorauf, "Extra-legal Political Parties in Wisconsin," *American Political Science Review* 48, no. 3 (September 1954): 692–704, 692.

21. Quoted in Eldon Eisenach, *The Next Religious Establishment: National Identity and Political Theology in Post-Protestant America* (New York: Rowman and Littlefield, 2000), 116.

22. Quoted in Green, *Devil's Bargain*, 117.

23. Julie Hirschfield, "Trump, in Wake of Deal to Avoid a Shutdown Now, Calls for One Later," *New York Times*, May 2, 2017, https://www.nytimes.com/2017/05/02 /us/politics/good-shutdown-congress-trump.html.

24. Matt Grossmann, "Missing Conservatism? Just Wait for a Democratic President," *New York Times*, February 20, 2018, https://www.nytimes.com/2018/02/20 /opinion/trump-conservatism-republicans.html.

25. Grossmann, noting that Republicans' only victories are lowering taxes and building the military.

26. Two essays focused on what their authors characterize as conspiracism from the left today are McKay Coppins, "How the Left Lost Its Mind," *Atlantic Monthly*, July 2, 2017, https://www.theatlantic.com/politics/archive/2017/07/liberal-fever -swamps/530736/; and Colin Dickey, "The New Paranoia," *New Republic*, June 8, 2017, https://newrepublic.com/article/142977/new-paranoia-trump-election-turns -democrats-conspiracy-theorists.

27. "Partisanship and Political Animosity in 2016," Pew Research Center, June 22, 2016, http://www.people-press.org/2016/06/22/partisanship-and-political-animosity -in-2016/.

28. David Brooks, "Why Partyism Is Wrong," *New York Times*, October 28, 2017, https://www.nytimes.com/2014/10/28/opinion/david-brooks-why-partyism-is -wrong.html. This is in contrast to the era of open and moderate partisanship in the 1950s and 1960s, when few cared whether their children married someone with an allegiance to the opposite party. Gabriel Almond and Sidney Verba, *The Civic Culture* (Princeton, NJ: Princeton University Press, 1963).

29. "Partisanship and Political Animosity."

Chapter 5. Knowledge

1. Brendan Nyhan, "Why the 'Death Panel' Myth Wouldn't Die: Misinformation in the Health Care Reform Debate," *Forum* 8, no. 1 (2010): Article 5, https://www.degruyter.com/view/j/for.2010.8.1_20120105083456/for.2010.8.1/for.2010.8.1.1354/for.2010.8.1.1354.xml.

2. Paul Krugman, "Facts Are Enemies of the People," *New York Times*, March 13, 2017, https://www.nytimes.com/2017/03/13/opinion/facts-are-enemies-of-the-people.html.

3. Tina Nguyen, "Trump Smears 3,000 Dead Puerto Ricans, Calls Hurricane Maria Death Toll a Democratic Hoax," *Vanity Fair*, September 13, 2018, https://www.vanityfair.com/news/2018/09/trump-death-toll-puerto-rico-democrat-hoax.

4. Michael E. Miller, "The GOP's Dangerous 'Debate' on Vaccines and Autism," *Washington Post*, September 17, 2015, http://www.washingtonpost.com/news/morning-mix/wp/2015/09/17/the-gops-dangerous-debate-on-vaccines-and-autism/.

5. Joshua Zeitz, "Lessons from the Fake News Pandemic of 1942," *Politico Magazine*, March 12, 2017, https://www.politico.com/magazine/story/2017/03/lessons-from-the-fake-news-pandemic-of-1942-214898.

6. "Meet the Press 01/22/17," full text, NBC News, January 22, 2017, https://www.nbcnews.com/meet-the-press/meet-press-01-22-17-n710491.

7. Ashley Parker and Steve Eder, "Inside the Six Weeks Donald Trump Was a Nonstop 'Birther,'" *New York Times*, July 2, 2016, https://www.nytimes.com/2016/07/03/us/politics/donald-trump-birther-obama.html.

8. Brian Tashman, "58 Donald Trump Conspiracy Theories (and Counting): The Definitive Donald Trump Conspiracy Guide," Right Wing Watch, May 27, 2016, http://www.rightwingwatch.org/post/58-donald-trump-conspiracy-theories-and-counting-the-definitive-trump-conspiracy-guide/.

9. Jennifer L. Hochschild and Katherine Levine Einstein, *Do Facts Matter? Information and Misinformation in American Politics* (Norman: University of Oklahoma Press, 2015), 113, 108–9.

10. Glenn Thrush and Maggie Haberman, "Trump Aides Address His Wiretap Claims: 'That's above My Pay Grade,'" *New York Times*, March 7, 2017, https://www.nytimes.com/2017/03/07/us/politics/trump-wiretap-claim-obama.html.

11. Jon Cohen, "Poll: Number of 'Birthers' Plummets," *Washington Post*, May 5, 2011, https://www.washingtonpost.com/blogs/behind-the-numbers/post/number-of-birthers-plummets/2011/05/04/AF3GAZxF_blog.html?utm_term=.02b5fdeab3bd.

12. Eugene Kiely, "Trump Surrogates Spin 'Birther' Narrative," FactCheck.org, September 19, 2016, https://www.factcheck.org/2016/09/trump-surrogates-spin-birther-narrative/.

13. Donald J. Trump (@realDonaldTrump), Twitter, December 12, 2013, 1:32 p.m., https://twitter.com/realdonaldtrump/status/411247268763676673?lang=en.

14. Tim Murphy, "How Donald Trump Became Conspiracy Theorist in Chief," *Mother Jones*, November–December 2016, https://www.motherjones.com/politics

/2016/10/trump-infowars-alex-jones-clinton-conspiracy-theories/; Maggie Haberman and Alan Rappeport, "Trump Drops False 'Birther' Theory but Starts a New One: Clinton Started It," *New York Times*, September 16, 2016, https://www.nytimes.com /2016/09/17/us/politics/donald-trump-birther-obama.html.

15. Jeffrey Kluger, "Senator Throws Snowball! Climate Change Disproven," *Time*, February 27, 2015, http://time.com/3725994/inhofe-snowball-climate/.

16. Tashman, "58 Donald Trump Conspiracy Theories."

17. Austin Ramzy, "Does Praise for China Make Group a 'Foreign Agent'? Republicans Say It Might," June 7, 2018, *New York Times*, https://www.nytimes.com/2018 /06/07/world/asia/natural-resources-defense-council-china.html.

18. Donald Trump, "President Trump on Christine Blasey Ford, His Relationships with Vladimir Putin and Kim Jong Un, and More," interview by Lesley Stahl, *60 Minutes*, October 14, 2018, https://www.cbsnews.com/news/donald-trump-full-interview -60-minutes-transcript-lesley-stahl-2018-10-14.

19. Naomi Oreskes and Eric Conway, *Merchants of Doubt: How a Handful of Scientists Obscured the Truth on Issues from Tobacco Smoke to Global Warming* (London: Bloomsbury, 2011), 6–7.

20. David Kaiser and Lee Wasserman, "The Rockefeller Family Fund Vs Exxon," *New York Review of Books*, December 8, 2016, https://www.nybooks.com/articles /2016/12/08/the-rockefeller-family-fund-vs-exxon/. See also Coral Davenport and Eric Lipton, "How G.O.P. Leaders Came to View Climate Change as Fake Science," *New York Times*, June 3, 2017, https://www.nytimes.com/2017/06/03/us/politics /republican-leaders-climate-change.html.

21. Riley E. Dunlap and Peter J. Jacques, "Climate Change Denial Books and Conservative Think Tanks," *American Behavioral Scientist* 57, no. 6 (June 2013): 699–731; Geoffrey Supran and Naomi Oreskes, "What Exxon Mobil Didn't Say about Climate Change," *New York Times*, August 22, 2017, https://www.nytimes.com/2017/08/22 /opinion/exxon-climate-change-.html; Naomi Oreskes and Geoffrey Supran, "Yes, ExxonMobil Misled the Public," *Los Angeles Times*, September 1, 2017, http://www .latimes.com/opinion/op-ed/la-oe-oreskes-supran-exxonmobil-20170901-story.html.

22. Quoted in Bill McKibben, "The Koch Brothers' New Brand," review of *Dark Money: The History of the Billionaires behind the Rise of the Radical Right*, by Jane Mayer, *New York Review of Books*, March 10, 2016, http://www.nybooks.com/articles/2016 /03/10/koch-brothers-new-brand/.

23. Davenport and Lipton, "How G.O.P. Leaders."

24. Nick Buxton, "The Military Is Resisting Trump's Denialism, but It's Still Not a Force for Climate Justice," Truthout, April 4, 2017, http://www.truth-out.org/news /item/40082-the-military-is-resisting-trumps-denialism-but-its-still-not-a-force-for -climate-justice.

25. John Schwartz, "A Leading Climate Agency May Lose Its Climate Focus," *New York Times*, June 23, 2018, https://www.nytimes.com/2018/06/24/climate/noaa -climate-mission.html.

26. Bill McKibben, "A March for the Future," *Nation*, May 8–15, 2017, 13.

27. Anthony Gaughan, "Illiberal Democracy: The Toxic Mix of Fake News, Hyperpolarization, and Partisan Election Administration," *Duke Journal of Constitutional Law and Public Policy* 12, no. 3 (2017): 59–139.

28. David M. J. Lazer et al., "The Science of Fake News," *Science* 369, no. 6380 (March 2018): 1094–96.

29. Aaron Blake, "InfoWars Is behind President Trump's Idea That the Media Is Covering Up Terrorist Attacks," *Washington Post*, February 6, 2017, https://www.washingtonpost.com/news/the-fix/wp/2017/02/06/trumps-suggestion-that-the-media-is-ignoring-terrorist-attacks-has-a-familiar-source-infowars/?utm_term=.f43a20952410; Jeremy W. Peters, "The Right Builds an Alternative Narrative about the Crises around Trump," *New York Times*, May 17, 2017, https://www.nytimes.com/2017/05/17/us/politics/trump-scandal-conservatives-media.html.

30. Calculated from the "Trump Twitter Archive," accessed September 18, 2018, http://www.trumptwitterarchive.com/archive/fake news || fakenews || fake media /ttff/1-19-2017.

31. David A. Bell, "Fake News Is Not the Real Media Threat We're Facing," *Nation*, December 22, 2016, https://www.thenation.com/article/fake-news-is-not-the-real-media-threat-were-facing/.

32. Donald J. Trump (@realDonaldTrump), Twitter, February 24, 2017, 10:09 p.m., https://twitter.com/realdonaldtrump/status/835325771858251776?lang=en.

33. Nolan D. McCaskill, "Trump Backs Bannon: 'The Media Is the Opposition Party,'" Politico, January 27, 2017, http://www.politico.com/story/2017/01/donald-trump-steve-bannon-media-opposition-party-234280.

34. Andrew Guess, Brendan Nyhan, and Jason Reifler, *You're Fake News! Findings from the Poynter Media Trust Survey* (Saint Petersburg, FL: Poynter Institute, November 29, 2017), https://poyntercdn.blob.core.windows.net/files/PoynterMedia-TrustSurvey2017.pdf.

35. Colleen Shalby, "Trump Calls 'Fake News' Media an Enemy of the People," *Los Angeles Times*, February 17, 2017, http://www.latimes.com/politics/washington/la-na-essential-washington-updates-donald-trump-called-fake-news-media-1487377442-htmlstory.html.

36. Jonathan Easley, "Trump: Media Is 'Scum,'" *Hill*, December 7, 2015, http://thehill.com/blogs/ballot-box/presidential-races/262400-trump-media-is-scum.

37. Theodore Schleifer, "Donald Trump on Reporters: I Would Never Kill Them," CNN Politics, December 21, 2015, https://www.cnn.com/2015/12/21/politics/trump-putin-killing-reporters/index.html.

38. Avi Selk and Kristine Phillips, "Watergate Reporter Carl Bernstein: Trump's Attacks on the Press Are More Dangerous than Nixon's," *Washington Post*, February 19, 2018, https://www.washingtonpost.com/news/the-fix/wp/2017/02/19/watergate-reporter-carl-bernstein-trumps-attacks-on-the-press-are-more-dangerous-than-nixons.

39. Bret Stephens, "Don't Dismiss President Trump's Attack on the Media as Mere Stupidity," Daniel Pearl Memorial Lecture, *Time*, last updated February 26, 2017, http://time.com/4675860/donald-trump-fake-news-attacks/?curator=MediaREDEF.

40. Sara Fischer, "92% of Republicans Think Media Intentionally Reports Fake News," Axios, July 9, 2018, https://www.axios.com/trump-effect-92-percent-republicans-media-fake-news-9c1bbf70-0054-41dd-b506-0869bb10f08c.html.

41. Charles Sykes, "Why Nobody Cares the President Is Lying," *New York Times*, February 4, 2017, https://www.nytimes.com/2017/02/04/opinion/sunday/why-nobody-cares-the-president-is-lying.html.

42. Hochschild and Einstein, *Do Facts Matter?*

43. Jodi Dean, "Theorizing Conspiracy Theory," *Theory and Event* 4, no. 3 (2000) 1–10: 2, 6.

44. Kate Starbird, "Information Wars: A Window into the Alternative Media Ecosystem," Medium, March 14, 2017, https://medium.com/hci-design-at-uw/information-wars-a-window-into-the-alternative-media-ecosystem-a1347f32fd8f.

45. Starbird; Danah Boyd, "You Think You Want Media Literacy . . . Do You?," Medium, March 9, 2018, https://points.datasociety.net/you-think-you-want-media-literacy-do-you-7cad6af18ec2.

46. Steve Kolowich, "The Water Next Time: Professor Who Helped Expose Crisis in Flint Says Public Science Is Broken," *Chronicle of Higher Education*, February 2, 2016, https://www.chronicle.com/article/The-Water-Next-Time-Professor/235136.

47. Z. Pamuk, "Examining the Experts: Science, Values, and Democracy" (PhD diss., Harvard University, 2017).

48. Pamuk.

49. Quoted in Frederick A. O. Schwarz Jr., *Democracy in the Dark: The Seduction of Government Secrecy* (New York: New Press, 2015), 110.

50. David Leonhardt, "The Original Lie about Obama Care," *New York Times*, March 14, 2017, https://www.nytimes.com/2017/03/14/opinion/the-original-lie-about-obamacare.html.

51. Steven Erlanger, "'Fake News,' Trump's Obsession, Is Now a Cudgel for Strongmen," *New York Times*, December 12, 2017, https://www.nytimes.com/2017/12/12/world/europe/trump-fake-news-dictators.html.

Chapter 6. Who Owns Reality?

1. George F. Will, "Trump Has a Dangerous Disability," *Washington Post*, May 3, 2017, https://www.washingtonpost.com/opinions/trump-has-a-dangerous-disability/2017/05/03/56ca6118-2f6b-11e7-9534-00e4656c22aa_story.html.

2. Hannah Arendt, "Understanding and Politics (The Difficulties of Understanding)," in *Essays in Understanding, 1930–1954*, ed. Jerome Kohn (New York: Schocken Books, 1994), 308, 310, 314. "The actual fight against totalitarianism needs no more than a steady flow of reliable information" (323n2).

3. *Oxford English Dictionary Online*, s.v. "common sense," accessed September 28, 2018, http://www.oed.com/view/Entry/37255.

4. Thomas L. Friedman, "Get out of Facebook and into the NRA's Face," *New York Times*, February 20, 2018, https://www.nytimes.com/2018/02/20/opinion/get-out-of -facebook-and-into-the-nras-face.html.

5. Tim Murphy, "How Donald Trump Became Conspiracy Theorist in Chief," *Mother Jones*, November–December 2016, https://www.motherjones.com/politics /2016/10/trump-infowars-alex-jones-clinton-conspiracy-theories/.

6. Pierre Bourdieu quoted in Sophia Rosenfeld, *Common Sense: A Political History* (Cambridge, MA: Harvard University Press, 2011), 256.

7. Arendt, "Understanding and Politics," 318

8. Arendt, 308, 310, 314.

9. Sabrina Tavernise and Katharine Q. Seelye, "Political Divide Splits Relationships—and Thanksgiving Too," *New York Times*, November 15, 2016, https://www.nytimes .com/2016/11/16/us/political-divide-splits-relationships-and-thanksgiving-too.html.

10. Quotations from the "research" welcome page on the message board 8chan, where participants post and discuss their analysis. "Welcome to /QResearch/," 8chan, accessed September 19, 2018, https://8ch.net/qresearch/welcome.html.

11. For instance, on August 3, 2018 the authors consulted the discussion of "clues" by QAnon researchers on the following Reddit.com message board: https://www .reddit.com/r/greatawakening/comments/84sam4/does_anyone_have_the_link_to _the_current_8chan/. A feature of this company of conspiracists is its avowed "masculinity." Posting is anonymous, and any female participants are encouraged to disguise their gender. As of September 12, 2018, the QAnon boards have been taken down by Reddit.com; see Brian Feldman, "Reddit Bans QAnon Hive," *New York Magazine*, September 12, 2018, accessed September 18, 2018 at http://nymag.com/selectall/2018 /09/reddit-bans-major-qanon-message-board-r-greatawakening.html.

12. Justin Bank, Leon Stack, and Daniel Victor, "What Is QAnon: Explaining the Internet Conspiracy That Showed Up at a Trump Rally," *New York Times*, August 1, 2018, https://www.nytimes.com/2018/08/01/us/politics/what-is-qanon.html.

13. Bandy Zadrozny and Ben Collins, "How Three Conspiracy Theorists Took 'Q' and Sparked Qanon," NBC News, August 14, 2018, https://www.nbcnews.com/tech /tech-news/how-three-conspiracy-theorists-took-q-sparked-qanon-n900531.

14. Tim Smith-Laing, "Following QAnon into the Age of Post-post Truth," *Economist*, August 14, 2018, https://www.1843magazine.com/people/what-just-happened /following-qanon-into-the-age-of-postposttruth.

15. Robin Grey, "Enlightenment and Scottish Common Sense Philosophy," in *The Oxford Handbook of Transcendentalism*, ed. Sandra Harbert Petrulionis, Laura Dassow Walls, and Joel Myerson (New York: Oxford University Press, 2012).

16. Rosenfeld, *Common Sense*, 2.

17. Thomas Paine, *Rights of Man, Common Sense, and Other Political Writings*, ed. Mark Philp (Oxford: Oxford University Press, 2009), 93, 27.

18. Paine, *Rights of Man, Common Sense, and Other Political Writings*, 23.

19. We owe this observation to a conversation with Corey Brettschneider.

20. Gordon Wood, "Creating the Revolution," review of Bernard Bailyn's work, *New York Review of Books*, February 13, 2003.

Chapter 7. Speaking Truth

1. As Pierre Rosanvallon argues, transparency means many things: it is a utopia in which citizens can see their officials' motivations all the way through; it is an ideology that promises to cure all the discontents that come with being governed; and, in a very concrete way, it is a mode of accountability. Pierre Rosanvallon, *Good Government: Democracy beyond Elections*, trans. Malcolm DeBevoise (Cambridge, MA: Harvard University Press, 2018), 246.

2. Scott Horton, *Lords of Secrecy: The National Security Elite and America's Stealth Warfare* (New York: Nation Books, 2015); *Examining the Costs of Overclassification on Transparency and Security: Hearing before the House Committee on Oversight and Government Reform* (December 7, 2016), https://oversight.house.gov/hearing/examining -costs-overclassification-transparency-security/.

3. For a nuanced discussion of transparency from which we draw, see Jonathan R. Bruno, "Democracy beyond Disclosure: Secrecy, Transparency, and the Logic of Self-Government" (PhD diss., Harvard University, 2017).

4. Onora O'Neill, "Ethics for Communication?," *European Journal of Philosophy* 17, no. 2 (2009): 167–80, 173.

5. Brendan Nyhan et al., "Classified or Coverup: The Effects of Redactions on Conspiracy Theory Beliefs," *Journal of Experimental Political Science* 3, no. 2 (Winter 2016): 109–23.

6. Rosanvallon, *Good Government*, 161–70.

7. Complicating the straightforward analogy to partisan voting, the Jade Helm 15 map colored Arizona (which had voted Republican in 2008 and 2012) light blue for "uncertain leaning friendly," and New Mexico (which had voted Democratic in 2008 and 2012) was colored brown for "uncertain leaning hostile."

8. Heather Digby Parton, "Right-Wing Lunatics Think the Military Is Planning to Invade Texas: Here's Why," Salon, April 30, 2015, https://www.salon.com/2015/04/30 /right_wing_lunatics_think_the_military_is_planning_to_invade_texas_heres_why/.

9. Patrick Svitek, "Abbott's Letter Elevates Jade Helm 15 Concerns," *Texas Tribune*, April 30, 2015, http://www.texastribune.org/2015/04/30/abbotts-letter-puts-jade -helm-national-stage/.

10. See "Fear and Absent Danger," *The Daily Show with Jon Stewart*, May 4, 2015, http://www.cc.com/video-clips/c54ewk/the-daily-show-with-jon-stewart-to-shoot -or-not-to-shoot—fear-and-absent-danger.

11. Louie Gohmert, "Gohmert Statement on Jade Helm Exercises," official website of Louie Gohmert, May 5, 2015, http://gohmert.house.gov/news/email/show .aspx?ID=RARJ62LPUKCT7BNM7ZBA3QA2VM.

12. John Council, "Lawyer's 'Pandering to Idiots' Letter Goes Viral," *Texas Lawyer*, May 7, 2015, http://www.texaslawyer.com/id=1202725781705/Lawyers-Pandering-to-Idiots-Letter-to-Abbott-Goes-Viral.

13. "Full Transcript: Jeff Flake's Speech on the Senate Floor," *New York Times*, October 24, 2017, https://www.nytimes.com/2017/10/24/us/politics/jeff-flake-transcript-senate-speech.html.

14. Daniel Bice, "Senator Ron Johnson Says an Informant Told Congress There Are Secret Anti-Trump Meetings in FBI," *Milwaukee Journal Sentinel*, January 23, 2018, https://www.jsonline.com/story/news/2018/01/23/sen-johnson-says-informant-alleges-secret-anti-trump-meetings-fbi/1060586001/.

15. "GOP Senator: 'Real Possibility' That FBI 'Secret Society' Text Was a Joke," *Hill*, January 25, 2018, http://thehill.com/homenews/senate/370707-ron-johnson-its-a-real-possibility-that-ex-fbi-agents-secret-society-text-was.

16. Laura Meckler, "McCain Asks Supporters to Show Obama Respect," *Wall Street Journal*, October 12, 2008, https://www.wsj.com/articles/SB122368132195924869.

17. "Full Transcript: Jeff Flake's Speech."

18. The phrase is from Robert Jay Lifton, *The Climate Swerve: Reflections on Mind, Hope, and Survival* (New York: New Press, 2017), 93.

19. Steven Levitsky and Daniel Ziblatt, *How Democracies Die* (New York: Crown, 2018), 189, 188.

20. David Runciman, *The Confidence Trap* (Princeton, NJ: Princeton University Press, 2013).

21. Cass R. Sunstein and Adrian Vermeule, "Conspiracy Theories: Causes and Cures," *Journal of Political Philosophy* 17, no. 2 (2009): 202–27, 219, 204, 221. Sunstein later reflected on some of the inadequacies of the Sunstein-Vermeule argument in Andrew Marantz, "How a Liberal Scholar of Conspiracy Theories Became the Subject of a Right-Wing Conspiracy Theory," *The New Yorker*, December 27, 2017, https://www.newyorker.com/culture/persons-of-interest/how-a-liberal-scholar-of-conspiracy-theories-became-the-subject-of-a-right-wing-conspiracy-theory.

22. United States Senate, *Intelligence Activities and the Rights of Americans*, bk. 2, *Final Report of the Select Committee to Study Governmental Operations with Respect to Intelligence Activities* (Washington, DC: Government Printing Office, April 26, 1976), 10–13, https://www.intelligence.senate.gov/sites/default/files/94755_II.pdf.

23. Quoted in Jeremy W. Peters, "Wielding Claims of 'Fake News,' Conservatives Take Aim at Mainstream Media," *New York Times*, December 25, 2016, https://www.nytimes.com/2016/12/25/us/politics/fake-news-claims-conservatives-mainstream-media-.html.

24. "Enforcing Our Community Standards," Facebook Newsroom, August 6, 2018, https://newsroom.fb.com/news/2018/08/enforcing-our-community-standards/.

25. "Enforcing Our Community Standards."

26. Sam Leith, "Nothing like the Truth," *Times Literary Supplement*, August 16, 2017, https://www.the-tls.co.uk/articles/public/post-truth-sam-leith/.

27. Brendan Nyhan and Jason Reifler, "When Corrections Fail: The Persistence of Political Misperceptions," *Political Behavior* 32, no. 2 (June 2010): 303–30.

28. See Charles J. Sykes, "The Danger of Ignoring Alex Jones," *New York Times*, June 17, 2017, https://www.nytimes.com/2017/06/17/opinion/sunday/the-danger-of-ignoring-alex-jones.html.

29. Thomas Wood and Ethan Porter, "The Elusive Backfire Effect: Mass Attitudes' Steadfast Factual Adherence," *Political Behavior* (forthcoming), last revised January 2, 2018, https://papers.ssrn.com/sol3/papers.cfm?abstract_id=2819073.

30. Brendan Nyhan and Jason Reifler, "The Effect of Fact-Checking on Elites: A Field Experiment on U.S. State Legislators," *American Journal of Political Science* 59, no. 3 (July 2015): 628–40; Brendan Nyhan and Jason Reifler, "Do People Actually Learn from Fact Checking? Evidence from a Longitudinal Study from the 2014 Campaign," November 30, 2016, http://www.dartmouth.edu/~nyhan/fact-checking-effects.pdf.

31. Eve Kosofsky Sedgwick, *Touching, Feeling: Affect, Pedagogy, Performativity* (Durham, NC: Duke University Press, 2003), 141.

32. Ari Berman, "The Man behind Trump's Voter-Fraud Obsession," *New York Times*, June 13, 2017, https://www.nytimes.com/2017/06/13/magazine/the-man-behind-trumps-voter-fraud-obsession.html.

33. David Cottrell, Michael C. Herron, and Sean J. Westwood, "An Exploration of Donald Trump's Allegations of Massive Voter Fraud in the 2016 General Election," August 23, 2017, http://www-personal.umich.edu/~dcott/pdfs/fraud_draft.pdf.

34. Berman, "Man behind Trump's."

35. David Weigel, "Election Integrity Commission Members Accuse New Hampshire Voters of Fraud," *Washington Post*, September 8, 2017, https://www.washingtonpost.com/news/powerpost/wp/2017/09/08/election-integrity-commission-members-accuse-new-hampshire-voters-of-fraud/?utm_term=.d293c18abadc.

36. This is how the *Kansas City Star* editorial board characterized the work of Trump's Presidential Advisory Commission on Election Integrity. See "Why Has Kris Kobach's Voter Fraud Commission Disappeared?," editorial, *Kansas City Star*, November 1, 2017, http://www.kansascity.com/opinion/editorials/article182150656.html.

37. Mark Berman and John Wagner, "Almost Every State Resists Trump's Voter Fraud Commission," *Chicago Tribune*, July 5, 2017, http://www.chicagotribune.com/news/nationworld/politics/ct-most-states-resist-voter-fraud-commission-20170705-story.html.

38. Dan Merica, "Trump Labels U.S. Justice System a 'Laughingstock,'" CNN, November 1, 2017, http://www.cnn.com/2017/11/01/politics/trump-justice-laughing-stock/index.html.

39. *The Situation Room*, full transcript, November 1, 2017, http://transcripts.cnn.com/TRANSCRIPTS/1711/01/sitroom.01.html.

40. "New York City Terror Attack News Conference," C-SPAN, November 1, 2017, https://www.c-span.org/video/?436710-1/york-city-terror-attack-news-conference.

41. Nicholas Fandos, "F.B.I. Agent Defends Actions in Russia Inquiry in Contentious House Testimony," *New York Times*, July 12, 2018, https://www.nytimes.com/2018/07/12/us/politics/fbi-agent-house-republicans.html.

42. Fandos, "F.B.I. Agent Defends Actions." Strzok's evidence of his own professional responsibility was that he was one of the few people who knew about Russian interference in the election on behalf of Trump during the campaign yet did not expose this potentially explosive information to derail Trump.

43. See Rosanvallon, *Good Government*, 162–63, 245–51. As Rosanvallon writes, conflating legibility and transparency (as well as the several distinct meanings of transparency) "leads to confusions" (251).

Conclusion: The Crisis of Democracy

1. Roberto Stefan Foa and Yascha Mounk, "The Signs of Deconsolidation," *Journal of Democracy* 28, no. 1 (January 2017): 5–16, http://www.journalofdemocracy.org /article/signs-deconsolidation.

2. Data cited in William Galston, *Anti-pluralism: The Populist Threat to Liberal Democracy* (New Haven, CT: Yale University Press, 2018), 12. Galston provides an itemized list of populist sentiments and beliefs on p. 112.

3. The term invokes political scientists' preoccupation with democratization and its consolidation. Roberto Stefan Foa and Yascha Mounk, "The Danger of Deconsolidation," *Journal of Democracy* 27, no. 3 (July 2016): 5–17, https://www .journalofdemocracy.org/article/danger-deconsolidation-democratic-disconnect; Foa and Mounk, " Signs of Deconsolidation."

4. Among the best assessments of the signs of authoritarianism is Steven Levitsky and Daniel Ziblatt, *How Democracies Die* (New York: Crown, 2018), whose authors "offer a litmus test to help identify would-be autocrats" (6). For another trenchant example, see Benjamin Carter Hett, *The Death of Democracy* (New York: Henry Holt, 2018).

5. For an overview, see Nadia Urbinati, "Populism," *Annual Review of Political Science* 22 (forthcoming, 2019). See too Nadia Urbinati, *Democracy Disfigured: Opinion, Truth, and the People* (Cambridge, MA: Harvard University Press, 2014); Jan-Werner Müller, *What Is Populism?* (Philadelphia: University of Pennsylvania Press, 2016); Galston, *Anti-pluralism*; John B. Judis, *The Populist Explosion* (New York: Columbia Global Reports, 2016); and Frances McCall Rosenbluth and Ian Shapiro, *Responsible Parties: Saving Democracy from Itself* (New Haven, CT: Yale University Press, 2018).

6. David Runciman, *How Democracy Ends* (New York: Basic Books, 2018), 7.

7. Bill Chappell, "'I'm the Only One That Matters,' Trump Says of State Department Vacancies," National Public Radio, November 3, 2017, https://www.npr.org /sections/thetwo-way/2017/11/03/561797675/im-the-only-one-that-matters-trump -says-of-state-dept-job-vacancies.

8. Justin Wise, "What You're Seeing in the News 'Is Not What's Happening,'" *Hill*, July 24, 2018, http://thehill.com/homenews/administration/398606-trump-what -youre-seeing-in-the-news-is-not-whats-happening-inbox-x.

9. We have in mind an intensification of the disinclination to participate in or to pay attention to politics that is already a prominent tendency in what John Hibbing and Elizabeth Theiss-Morse call "stealth democracy." See John R. Hibbing and Elizabeth

Theiss-Morse, *Stealth Democracy: Americans' Beliefs about How Government Should Work* (New York: Cambridge University Press, 2002).

10. American Academy of Arts and Sciences, *Perceptions of Science in America* (Cambridge, MA: American Academy of Arts and Sciences, 2018), 3, https://www.amacad.org/content/publications/publication.aspx?d=43055.

11. Turkuler Isiksel, "Prepare for Regime Change, not Policy Change," *Dissent*, November 13, 2016, https://www.dissentmagazine.org/blog/trump-victory-regime-change-lessons-autocrats-erdogan-putin.

12. On the connection between "legibility" and conspiracism, see Pierre Rosan-vallon, *Good Government: Democracy beyond Elections*, trans. Malcolm DeBevoise (Cambridge, MA: Harvard University Press, 2018), 161–64.

13. Quoted in James Risen and Tom Risen, "Donald Trump Does His Best Joe McCarthy Impression," *New York Times*, June 22, 2017, https://www.nytimes.com/2017/20/22/opinion/sunday/donald-trump.

14. Archibald MacLeish quoted in Jill Lepore, "The World That Trump and Ailes Built," *New Yorker*, June 5 and 12, 2017, https://www.newyorker.com/magazine/2017/06/05/the-world-that-trump-and-ailes-built.

ACKNOWLEDGMENTS

We extended our work on political parties to the subject of conspiracism at the invitation of Alfred Moore and published our first article, "Speaking Truth to Conspiracy: Partisanship and Trust," for a 2016 volume Moore edited for *Critical Review*. We amplified our argument in a 2017 article, "The New Conspiracism and the Delegitimation of Democracy," at the invitation of Leo Casey for a special issue of *Dissent* magazine on the crisis of democracy. We are grateful for these opportunities.

Rob Tempio, our editor at Princeton University Press, was enthusiastic about the project from our earliest conversation over coffee at the Film Society of Lincoln Center café. He shepherded the manuscript through publication, peppered us with probing questions and useful quotes, and prodded us to meet a very tight deadline!

For editorial suggestions we thank Madeleine Adams and Ashley Moore. For help with research, we thank Avishay Ben Sasson-Gordis and Leah Downey.

Nancy Rosenblum is grateful to Robert Jay Lifton for sharing her preoccupation with the campaign, election, and presidency of Donald Trump. Our never-ending conversation about "malignant normality" was invaluable, and even a sort of balm.

Russell Muirhead thanks Toni Barry for her loving encouragement throughout and Margaret Muirhead for her hearty support and careful attention to several iterations of the manuscript.

INDEX

A NOTE ON THE TYPE

This book has been composed in Adobe Text and Gotham.
Adobe Text, designed by Robert Slimbach for Adobe,
bridges the gap between fifteenth- and sixteenth-century
calligraphic and eighteenth-century Modern styles.
Gotham, inspired by New York street signs, was designed
by Tobias Frere-Jones for Hoefler & Co.